# TORCH BIBLE
# COMMENTARIES

## General Editors

**THE REV. JOHN MARSH, D.PHIL.**
*Principal of Mansfield College, Oxford*

**THE REV. DAVID M. PATON, M.A.**
*Editor, SCM Press*

**THE REV. ALAN RICHARDSON, D.D.**
*Professor of Christian Theology in the University of Nottingham*

# FOREWORD TO SERIES

The aim of this series of commentaries on books of the Bible is to provide the general reader with the soundest possible assistance in understanding the message of each book considered as a whole and as a part of the Bible.

The findings and views of modern critical scholarship on the text of the Bible have been taken fully into account. Indeed, it is our view that only on a basis of sound scholarship can the message of the Bible be fully understood. But minute points of scholarship, of language or archaeology or text, have not been pushed into the foreground. We have asked the writers of the various books to have in mind the view that the Bible is more than a quarry for the practice of erudition; that it contains the living message of the living God.

The 'general' reader whom we wish to help is therefore not only of one type. We hope that intelligent people of varying interests will find that these commentaries, while not ignoring the surface difficulties, are able to concentrate the mind on the essential Gospel contained in the various books of the Bible. In brief, the TORCH BIBLE COMMENTARIES are for the thoughtful reader who wishes to understand his Bible.

Volumes in the series include:

# DEUTERONOMY

*Introduction and Commentary*

**BY**

## H. CUNLIFFE-JONES

**Principal**
**Yorkshire United Independent College**
**Bradford**

**SCM PRESS LTD**
**56 BLOOMSBURY STREET, LONDON WC1**

TO
# MY MOTHER
whose faith nourished me

*First published April 1951*
*Reprinted November 1956*

*Printed in Great Britain by*
BILLING & SONS LTD.
GUILDFORD AND LONDON

# CONTENTS

## COMMENTARY

5

## II

### THE SECOND SPEECH OF MOSES
### (5.1-11.32)

*The Covenant at Moab: a commentary
on the First Commandment* (6.1-11.32)

## VI

### TWO FORMS OF SERVICE FOR THE WORSHIP OF THE GOD OF ISRAEL
#### (26.1-15)

## VII

### THE COVENANT OBLIGATIONS OF GOD AND HIS PEOPLE    147
#### (26.16-19)

PART THREE.   The Blessing and the Curse (27.1-30.20)

## VIII

### THE LAW AND THE CURSES
#### (27.1-26)

# PREFACE

As I have read the works of the great Biblical scholars in preparation for writing this commentary, I have been brought to a new sense of the greatness and integrity of their achievement. They have given, and are still giving to us, a truer and richer historical understanding of the Bible, in general and in detail, than men have ever yet had.

But often their most illuminating insight into the religious meaning of the Bible is hidden from us in the forbidding complexities of technical scholarship. And often, too, they limit themselves to discovering the historical meaning of any passage and do not go on to ask: What, then, is its living word for us to-day? It is this question which, on the basis of an historical understanding, I have tried to answer in relation to the book of Deuteronomy. The commentary is based on the Authorized Version, and is meant for the general reader.

I am specially indebted to Professor H. H. Rowley, who read both Introduction and Commentary, and to Professor C. R. North, and Professor N. W. Porteous, who read the Introduction. I have profited by their suggestions. I am also indebted to various other friends who read and commented on all or part of the manuscript, the Revs. R. T. Brooks, W. D. Davies, James Stewart and R. R. Turner. I am grateful to Professor T. W. Manson for information on one particular point. I am much indebted to one of the editors of the series, Professor John Marsh, for his careful criticism. I owe much to Miss Dorothy Gill for her kindness and patience in typing the manuscript. I am grateful to the Rev. John Young for his help in proof-reading.

YORKSHIRE UNITED INDEPENDENT COLLEGE
BRADFORD
*December 1950*

# BIBLIOGRAPHY

*For a general Introduction* read:

W. O. E. OESTERLEY and T. H. ROBINSON. *Introduction to the Books of the Old Testament.* S.P.C.K. 1934.

H. H. ROWLEY. *The Growth of the Old Testament.* Hutchinson 1950.

> The Prophet Jeremiah and the Book of Deuteronomy in *Studies in Old Testament Prophecy* presented to Professor T. H. Robinson. T. & T. Clark 1950.

JOHN SKINNER—the chapter on ' Jeremiah and Deuteronomy ' in *Prophecy and Religion.* Cambridge University Press 1922.

C. R. NORTH—the chapter on ' The Deuteronomists ' in *The Old Testament Interpretation of History.* Epworth Press 1946.

D. R. SCOTT. ' Deuteronomy ' in *The Abingdon Bible Commentary.* Epworth Press 1932.

*The greatest expositor in English* is A. C. Welch. The reason for this is that he treats the book as part of the living faith of Israel. His limitations are that he is not always right in his literary and historical judgments, and that, while he can write very simply on the issues of faith, he passes from general discussion to treatment of abstruse technical details without any consideration for the reader.

A. C. WELCH.—the chapter on ' Deuteronomy ' in *The Religion of Israel under the Kingdom.* T. & T. Clark 1912.

> *The Code of Deuteronomy.* James Clarke 1924.
>
> *Jeremiah: His Time and Work.* Oxford University Press 1928 (2nd ed. Blackwell 1951).
>
> *Deuteronomy: The Framework to the Code.* Oxford University Press 1932.

*Commentaries:*

S. R. DRIVER. 'Deuteronomy' *International Critical Commentary 1895*—the largest full-scale commentary, on which all later work depends. It is a fine work, and well written.

H. WHEELER ROBINSON. 'Deuteronomy and Joshua' *Century Bible 1907*—a masterly summary of scholarly facts useful to the study of the history of religion.

GEORGE ADAM SMITH. 'Deuteronomy' *Cambridge Bible 1918*—this book contains too great a burden of purely factual information. But its occasional flashes of religious insight are invaluable.

# WHAT IS DEUTERONOMY?

George Adam Smith wrote at the end of the introduction to his commentary: 'While so nobly serving its own age and establishing a discipline that with all its limitations—and indeed partly because of these—preserved and trained Israel for their mission to mankind, Deuteronomy gives utterance to truths which are always and everywhere sovereign—that God is One, and that man is wholly His, that it is He who finds us rather than we who find Him; that God is Righteousness and Faithfulness, Mercy and Love, and that these also are what He requires from us towards Himself and one another; that His will lies not in any unknown height but in the moral sphere known and understood by all (30.11-14). Thus in the preparation for Jesus Christ, Deuteronomy stands very high. Did He not Himself attest the divine authority both of its doctrine and of its style by accepting its central Creed as the highest and ultimate law not for Israel only but for all mankind (Mark 12.28-30, Deut. 6.4-5)?'

If this is right, or nearly right, then Deuteronomy must have a living message for us to-day and stand high among the books on which specially we can feed our souls. Yet many find it difficult and daunting. The reason must lie in that mixture of limitation and greatness which is characteristic of Deuteronomy.

George Adam Smith also wrote: 'The whole Israel is here, as in no other book of the Old Testament—the whole Israel in its limitations as in its potentiality, in its sins as in its aspirations, in its narrow fanatic tempers as in its vision and passion for the Highest.' And Professor S. A. Cook wrote:[1] 'One cannot too highly value the ethics of Deuteronomy, while deploring its narrowness; one must appreciate the part it played in inculcating generosity, while regretting its fanaticism.' A true appreciation of Deuteronomy will hold on to its greatness in spite of its limitations.

[1] *The Old Testament: a Reinterpretation*, 1936, p. 186.

15

The book of Deuteronomy is fundamentally a reinterpretation of the meaning of the Covenant of God with Israel under Moses to serve the life of Israel at a later time. The author—or, it may well be, authors—is concerned to link what he has to say with the Mosaic tradition, but he is primarily concerned that that tradition should not be lost but vindicated by being reaffirmed in the life of Israel in his own time.

The book has the qualities of a great sermon, and it is possible that it originated in liturgical expositions of the meaning of the Mosaic covenant. Certain it is that its distinctive style which, by its rolling tones, its adjectives, its repetitions, its affirmations, brings home the inner content of its message to the heart of the reader, has contributed something quite essential to the power of the Bible to speak the word of God to the minds of its readers.

> e.g. 10.17: 'For the Lord your God is God of gods, and Lord of lords, a great God, a mighty and a terrible, which regardeth not persons, nor taketh reward.'
> or 10.20: 'Thou shalt fear the Lord thy God; him shalt thou serve, and to him shalt thou cleave, and swear by his name.'

And this power of the language of preaching applies not simply to the addresses in the book. It applies also to the laws. The laws are not simply statute laws set down factually, precisely and unemotionally. They are 'preached laws'.[2] As George Adam Smith says: 'The style of the book is but the music of the winds that blow and sing through it alone—that sing even among its laws.' The laws are not only factual injunctions: they are also appeals to the conscience of the hearer.

> e.g. 14.22: 'Thou shalt truly tithe all the increase of thy seed that the field bringeth forth year by year.'
> 14.23: 'And thou shalt eat before the Lord thy God, in the place which he shalt choose to place his name there,

[2] cp. G. von Rad: *Deuteronomium-Studien*, Göttingen, 1948, p. 11.

the tithe of thy corn, of thy wine, and of thine oil, and the firstlings of thy herds and of thy flocks; that thou mayest learn to fear the Lord thy God always.'

Deuteronomy is a pleading with Israel to acknowledge Yahweh their God as their Covenant God, and to live as befits God's Covenant people. The Covenant rests on the accomplished redemption which God has brought about, it is due to his outpoured love and mercy that Israel has been given its life and destiny as a people. The future of Israel depends on their accepting this destiny from the hands of God and walking worthily of it.

In order to be effective, this pleading must be quite definite, and the thought of the Deuteronomist is expressed in terms of black and white. His is not an historical mind, for history would introduce all shades of grey and defeat the urgency of the appeal. What history is introduced is quite static in character, touching only fixed points, and is strictly subordinated to the main theme. The analogy of Deuteronomy in the New Testament is the Johannine literature. The strength of this type of mind is that where it is right it is gloriously and triumphantly right: its weakness is that where it is wrong, it is disastrously wrong.

## WHY SHOULD WE READ IT?

This commentary does not set out to answer all the questions which may be asked about the book of Deuteronomy. Those who are primarily interested in the historical meaning of Deuteronomy for its own time must look elsewhere. What this commentary seeks to do is to answer a question which is sometimes given insufficient attention: What is the religious meaning of Deuteronomy for a present-day religious reader? (This presupposes the historical study of the book and builds upon it.)

We should read Deuteronomy, then, for two reasons. First, to understand that background of God's revelation of himself to his people which the New Testament takes for granted and upon which it builds. We need to absorb the permanent meaning of the Divine discipline of Israel in order to appropriate rightly the New Testament revelation of God in Christ.

Secondly, to understand the application to a wider area of life and experience than that given in the New Testament, of a faith which, in spite of its limitations and distortions, is one with that faith in God created by God's redemption in Christ Jesus.

The centre of the Bible is the grace of God manifested in the life, death, and resurrection of Jesus Christ our Lord. We read that in the Gospels interpreted by the Epistles. We go to the Old Testament, not for what we know already from the New Testament, but for what the Old Testament tells us in its own right which is implied, but not stated, in the New.

But because when Deuteronomy was written Jesus Christ had not yet come, we must expect to find in it defects and distortions as well as true affirmations of faith.


## THE GREATNESS OF DEUTERONOMY

The greatness of Deuteronomy consists in that

### 1  It acknowledges God as God

For Israel, Yahweh, the God of Israel, has that personal moral character in majesty and sovereignty which constitutes Deity. (The fact that the teaching of the book is not at all points monotheistic is of small account compared with the fundamental recognition of Yahweh as God.) He is not to be represented in any material symbol. And he is to be feared, that is, given that utter reverence which is the proper attitude of man before God. Israel, therefore, must not worship other Gods, but keep strictly to the worship of the one true God.


### 2  It affirms the love of God

God has poured out upon Israel a love which they have not deserved. He has loved Israel, caring for them with a father's love for his son. He has delivered them from bondage in

Egypt and led them safely through the desert, and brought
them into the Promised Land.  Out of his great love he has
chosen them to be his people.

### 3  It insists that the response to God is love and obedience

Because God is the true God of Israel, Israel must obey his
commandments and keep steadfastly to his laws.  Only in
obeying God can Israel find life and blessing.  But this
obedience must carry with it the affection and devotion of
the whole heart.  The love of Israel for their God is the
right response to his redeeming love.  (This love of man for
God is distinctive of Deuteronomy.  Only once outside Deuteronomy in the Pentateuch (i.e. the first five books of the Bible)
is the love of man for God mentioned, and that (Ex. 20.6) may
be due to the influence of this book.)

### 4  It teaches that Israel is a holy people

God has chosen Israel to be his people, and the life of
Israel must exhibit the marks of that relationship.  Israel
must remember what God has done for them, and not forget
that they owe their distinctive life to God, or imitate the habits
of those who have not entered into this relationship.  A holy
God implies a holy people.

### 5  It claims that because God is God, human life shall be just and generous

There are drastic exceptions to what has been called the
'humanitarianism' of Deuteronomy: but if we leave them
out of account for the moment, then the characteristic social
teaching of Deuteronomy is an insistence on what is true
and upright, and a generous treatment of those who are in
need.  Both qualities in human life are the corollary of the
nature of Israel's God.  Because God is God, the character
befitting his people is one of honest and upright dealing, and
because of their own experience in Egypt of what it means to
live in a foreign land, a generous concern for all who cannot
themselves enforce their own rights.

**6   It is confident of the triumph of God's reign**

The foundation of Deuteronomy is a serene confidence that
this is God's world and that his will is completely effective.
With God is life: apart from him is death.  Obedience to God
is blessing: disobedience means curse and destruction.  The
doxology to the Lord's Prayer 'For thine is the Kingdom,
and the power, and the glory, for ever, Amen' expresses the
conviction of Deuteronomy.

**7   It is concerned for the transmission of faith to the younger
      generation**

In Deuteronomy the unit of religious faith is the family, and
it embodies a concern that the faith should be handed on
from generation to generation, which has been a permanent
source of strength in Judaism and Christianity.

**8   It is a written document which could be accepted as a
      standard of faith**

It is important to recognize that the process, which ultimately
led to the official acknowledgement of that collection of
authoritative writings which we call the Canon of the Old
Testament, began with the acceptance of the Book of Deuteronomy.  We cannot attribute to the author or authors of
Deuteronomy complete certainty that this would happen.  But
it is an authoritative interpretation of the meaning of Israel's
history—meant to guard against their falling below the victory
of faith already won.  If we believe that present relationship
with the living God needs renewal from the creative centre of
his revelation, we must see, in this character of the book, a
gift of God.

**9   It thinks of ritual in terms of God's purpose for Israel**

We are bound to put the concern of Deuteronomy in the
matter of ritual on both the credit and debit side of the book.
On the one hand, the acknowledgement of the place that ritual
plays in the maintenance of the life of a religious community
is right, and so, too, is the concern that this should witness to
the one true God, and should be a means of ensuring that he,

and he alone is worshipped. On the other hand, the central-ization of worship in a fixed place makes it almost inevitable that the understanding of worship which it produces will be too national, too rigid, and too formal. The fact that the institutional expression of the faith of Deuteronomy is the source of great good and of great harm is fundamental to our understanding of the worth of the book.

## THE LIMITATIONS OF DEUTERONOMY

The limitations of Deuteronomy consist in that

**1  It is ruthless in its laws against worshippers of other gods**
The principle which Deuteronomy lays down is that all worshippers of other gods within the land of Israel must be exterminated. Historically the command was not in force till the Israelites had been in Canaan for some centuries, and the injunction was meant to remove those elements of Canaan-ite tradition which might destroy the distinctive inhèritance of Israel. But it is a serious blemish against the permanent importance of Deuteronomy that it has not learnt to combine a passionate faith in the one true God who is the central loyalty of all men with tolerance towards the persons of those who mistakenly or wickedly worship other gods. But this is a lesson which men have been slow to learn (see Reinhold Niebuhr: *The Nature and Destiny of Man*, vol. II, chap. viii).

**2  It is harsh in its methods of removing evil from the community**
In dealing with evil in the community Deuteronomy applies the principle of equal retribution (cp. 19.16-21), and demands the death penalty for a large number of offences, not only for murder (19.11-13) but also for the revolt of sons against parents (21.18-21) sexual intercourse outside marriage (22.20-21), adultery (22.22), selling an Israelite as a slave (24.7). There may be historical reasons (such as absence of prisons) which explain these drastic measures: but they are a blemish on the

permanent worth of Deuteronomy as a guide to human action. Harshness is no guarantee of the removal of evil from community life.

### 3 It believes that suffering is directly the result of disobedience to God

The main Deuteronomic idea of the moral government of the universe is simple and clear: prosperity is the result of obedience to God; adversity is the result of disobeying him. This is mitigated only by one passage on the disciplinary function of suffering (8.2-5). The Deuteronomist is right in his main conviction that to go God's way means blessing, and to go against God's way means curse, but he has not learnt that men may inflict evil on others because of their goodness, that good men may need voluntarily to accept suffering for the sake of others, and that the vindication of the good and the defeat of evil is only partially seen in this life.

### 4 It believes that prosperity is directly the result of goodness

The Deuteronomist urges Israel to love and obey God for his own sake: the prosperity which this will bring is only a corollary. There is, however, some danger that the stress on immediate reward may be turned into the main motive. We cannot wholly escape this dilemma, because in God's universe God's way of life is supremely effective, but the reward is not immediate and is incidental to the love of God and the love of man.

### 5 It has a rigidity which forbids alteration

It is only an age much later than that of the Deuteronomists themselves which treats Deuteronomic injunctions as completely rigid, but the misunderstanding is based on the absolute character of its demands, and the injunctions not to add to it or take away from it. The central insight is fundamental to God's revelation of himself, but within that insight there must be room for change and growth.

### 6 It is a legal enforcement of religious reformation

Deuteronomy has often been unfairly compared with

Jeremiah, chap. 31, for the new covenant written in the heart
of man will only come fully with the consummation of Christ's
Kingdom.  But there are limits to what legal enactment can
do in the way of reformation, and Josiah's reformation, if
based on Deuteronomy, is not a good example of method for
the Church of God.  But the heart of Deuteronomic law is
not legal enactment, but a pleading for the generous heart.

## 7  It limits to Israel God's concern with all men

The Deuteronomist is rightly concerned with the meaning
of the people of God, but he limits this by picturing the ideal
Israel as the terror and envy of other nations, and by having
no missionary impulse. (Yet the inclusion of the stranger
within the family of Israel is a seed from which the missionary
impulse could grow.)  What is true in the teaching given of
God's Israel should be applied first to the Church and then to
all men.  The message of the book has a universal meaning
beyond its own perception.

## 8  It has no faith in life beyond death

If the great affirmations of Deuteronomy about God are
right, then God's Kingdom is an everlasting kingdom.  This
implication of his faith the Deuteronomist does not see, and
we must set his message in a wider framework than his own.
(Yet the belief in God as the giver of life contains the possibility of that wider faith.)

## NAME

The Hebrew text gives no name to the book: it was referred
to by its opening words: ' These are the words ' or ' Words.'
The Greek translators in 8.18 translated ' a copy of this law '
by *this second law-giving* (*deuteronomion*) which was adopted
as a title of the whole book.  While this is not wholly inap-
propriate, it fails to bring out the distinctive character of the
book.  It is a pity that the idea of ' law ' (Heb. *Torah*, instruction) was ever separated from its association with and depen-

dence on the richer idea of 'covenant'.[3]   If we had to name
the book we would call it something like 'The Preaching of
the Covenant'.

## DATE

1. Deuteronomy cannot have been written by Moses, in spite
of the statements in it that the laws (31.9) and the Song
(31.19) were written by him.   (a) The style of Deuteronomy is
distinctive among the traditions ascribed to Moses, and there
are irreconcilable differences among the laws of the Pentateuch;
(b) the death of Moses is narrated (34); (c) the formula ' unto
this day' (3.14, 10.8, 34.6) reveals that the author lived a long
time after Moses; (d) the land *east* of the Jordan is called the
land on *the other side* of the Jordan (1.1-15, 2.8, 4.46—so in
the R.V. correctly) which proves that the author lived in
Palestine, which Moses never entered.
2. But when was it written?   Scholars have not reached
complete agreement.   'From Deuteronomy,' it has been said,
' dates a whole new Epoch for Israel.   We must describe
Deuteronomy in every respect as the centre of the Old Testament.   Its origin is the most difficult question in the history
of Old Testament tradition.'[4]   The difficulty arises from the
facts that the dating has to be decided by internal evidence,
and that the book itself contains early, middle, and late
elements.   R. H. Pfeiffer has said:[5] 'Deuteronomy represents
the final result of a series of editorial expansions beginning in
621 and ending about 400 B.C.'   But to this must be added
that the original book written before 621 contained early
traditional material woven into the Deuteronomic purpose.
There is, then, some ground for a variety of opinions.
3. Most scholars since the studies of de Wette (1805) have
held the ancient view suggested by Athanasius, Chrysostom
and Jerome, that Deuteronomy (in part at least—possibly

      [3] cp. M. Noth: *Die Gesetze im Pentateuch: Ihre Voraussetzungen und
ihr Sinn*, 1940.
      [4] G. von Rad, *op. cit.*, p. 25.
      [5] *Introduction to the Old Testament*, 1941, p. 187.

5-26, 28) is the *basis for the reformation* under King Josiah
in 621 B.C., described in II Kings 22-23, ' The book of the covenant ' was found in the Temple, evidently containing preaching,
laws and curses. The main reforms were the centralization of
worship (II Kings 23.4, 5, 8, 12, 13, 15, 16, 19, cp. Deut. 12.1-7)
and the celebration of the Passover in the Temple and not at
home (II Kings 23.21-23, cp. Deut. 16.1-8). Detailed reforms
dealt with : the worship of the heavenly bodies (II Kings 23.4,
5, 11, cp. Deut. 17.3); the sacred poles and pillars (A.V. groves
and images; II Kings 23.4, 6, 7, 14, cp. Deut. 16.21-22, 12.3);
the sacrifice of children in the fire (II Kings 23.10, cp.
Deut. 18.10); sexual licence in worship (II Kings 23.7, cp.
Deut. 23.18); the practice of magic and divination (II Kings
23.24, cp. Deut. 18.11). It is important to note that the law of
Deut. 18.8 by which the country Levites were admitted to the
full privileges of priests was not carried out, and that the
narrative regrets this (II Kings 23.9). It seems exceedingly
likely, then, that the book which produced this effect was part
of our present book of Deuteronomy.

4. The date of Deuteronomy would, then, seem to lie in the
century or so before the reformation under King Josiah in
621 B.C.—either in the Northern Kingdom under the stimulus
of the prophetic movement of the eighth century, or in the
Southern Kingdom (though embodying many of the best
traditions of the Northern Kingdom, after the fall of Samaria
in 722) and written early in the long reign of Manasseh (692-
638) and forgotten. This general position seems likely to
command the assent of the majority of scholars.

5. If it is disputed, there seem to be three possibilities.
First, the account in Kings can be discounted as a reading
back into Josiah's reign of details which belong to a later
history. Josiah was killed at Megiddo in 608 B.C. and the
permanent effect of Deuteronomy is post-exilic. The centralization of worship is more appropriate to the conditions created
by the Exile, and it may perhaps be dated about 500 B.C.
This theory, associated especially with the names of G.
Hölscher and R. H. Kennett (though they approached the
problem differently) is unnecessarily sceptical of the record in

Kings. Even if this includes details which come from later
history, it is a straightforward account, and includes in the
prophecy of Huldah (II Kings 22.1-20) not only a pessimism
as to the outcome of the reformation (which is probably wisdom after the event), but also a prophecy of Josiah's personal
safety, which is certainly genuine.

6. A second possibility is that there was an early central-
ization of worship under Samuel which was disrupted and
Deuteronomy forgotten in the separation of the Kingdoms of
Israel and Judah. This theory is associated with the name of
Edward Robertson. There seems insufficient evidence to
justify it.

7. A third possibility is that centralization which bulks so
largely in the Josianic reformation, and in the Deuteronomic
judgment given in the history of the kingdoms, is not the determining conviction which produced Deuteronomy. That
determining conviction is faith in Yahweh as the one God of
Israel. Therefore, we can acknowledge in Deuteronomy
traditions (besides those of Ex. 20-23 (' The Book of the
Covenant ') which Deuteronomy adapts for its own purposes)
which go back a long way before 621 B.C. In particular, we
can do full justice to the book's association with the Northern
Kingdom. This theory is particularly associated with the
name of A. C. Welch. While particular arguments to limit
the influence of centralization have not won acceptance, the
recognition of early traditions and the association with the
Northern Kingdom are important, and can be combined with
the main theory. This can be seen in the work of the greatest
expositor of Deuteronomy in German: Gerhard von Rad.


## RELATION TO THE OTHER BOOKS OF
## THE BIBLE

It has been said of Deuteronomy,[6] ' Its influence on the
domestic and personal religion of all ages has never been

[6] George Adam Smith: *Modern Criticism and the Preaching of the Old
Testament*, p. 163.

exceeded by that of any other book in the Canon,' and within the Bible its influence has been very great.

## 1 The Pentateuch

The Pentateuch is a history of salvation from Abraham to the death of Moses, prefaced (Gen. 1-11) by expositions of the meaning of human life cast into story form. It thus contains preaching, narrative and laws. Scholars find in the Pentateuch three quite distinct documents: one embodying the traditions of the Southern and Northern Kingdoms (JE) which is early; the second, the Deuteronomic (D) which presupposes these traditions and builds upon them, and a later priestly style (P) which assumes the standpoint of Deuteronomy and develops the methods by which the distinctive life of Israel may be exhibited and maintained. Though some scholars now prefer to speak of strata of tradition rather than documents, this analysis of the Pentateuch is not likely ever to be shaken. Within the later priestly tradition there is distinguished the Holiness Code (H) (Lev. 17-26) which is probably a little later than Deuteronomy and in any case almost entirely independent.

To the narrative of the Pentateuch Deuteronomy adds nothing original but selects a few incidents to illustrate its teaching. In the laws we may note, in contrast with the early laws, the centralization of worship, a sharp denunciation of Canaanite customs, and a greater emphasis on justice and generosity as the conduct characteristic of those who are loyal to the God of Israel. In contrast with the later laws we may note that all members of the tribe of Levi are priests, not only those descended from Aaron, and that the elaborate ritual of Exodus-Leviticus (which forms the climax of revelation in the later source) is unknown. In contrast to both sets of laws, Deuteronomy includes a law warning of the dangers of kingship, and laws attempting to grapple with the nature of true prophecy.

## 2 The Prophets

The greatness of Deuteronomy comes from the fact that it

is an assimilation of the teaching of the eighth-century prophets
on a community basis, or else expresses the context of corporate conviction in which these same prophets did their work.
Attempts have been made to link Deuteronomy specially with
Hosea or with Isaiah—but it is best to acknowledge his indebtedness to all four—Amos, Hosea, Isaiah, Micah.[7] There
may be truth in the contention[8] that 'instead of being a pro-
gressive reform based on an advance beyond previous levels
of religion and cult it was a conscious effort to recapture both
the letter and the spirit of Mosaism which, the Deuteronomist
believed, had been neglected or forgotten by the Israelites of
the Monarchy.' But the emergence in Israel of this revived and
developed Mosaism, under the influence of the eighth-century
prophets was a new thing. The prophets had taught that God,
the sovereign Lord of history, was a God of righteousness, that
out of his great love he had entered into a special relation
with Israel. But because of his love he demands righteousness first of all from his chosen people. However few the
righteous remnant may be, it is to them God will give prosperity. And these truths Deuteronomy seeks to make the
basis of the whole life of Israel.

It is difficult to decide what is the true relation between
Deuteronomy and Jeremiah. It is probable, however, that
Jeremiah was influenced by Deuteronomy and not vice versa.
Jeremiah saw the limited influence of the actual reform and
hungered after the universal presence of the converted heart.
Ezekiel is a mediating influence between Deuteronomy and
the later priestly legislation. The great teaching of Deutero-
Isaiah influenced the revision of the book of Deuteronomy (cp.
with 4.15-40 Isaiah 44, 45) to enrich its teaching of the great-
ness of the God of Israel.

## 3  The Histories
There are three works of history in the Old Testament. One
is the Pentateuch in which the Priestly stratum supplies the

---

[7] cp. the useful table in H. Wheeler Robinson's *Deuteronomy and Joshua*,
Century Bible, pp. 33-4.
[8] W. F. Albright: *From the Stone Age to Christianity*, p. 244.

framework, but leaves the incorporated elements largely untouched; a second is Chronicles-Ezra-Nehemiah, in which the priestly stratum dominates its materials, though Chronicles itself has a Deuteronomic foundation; a third is the Deuteronomic work of history (in which some scholars include Deuteronomy itself), Joshua-Judges-Samuel-Kings, in which the Deuteronomic editor supplies the standpoint from which the material has been judged. In Joshua (in which there are mingled Deuteronomic and priestly elements), the influence of Deuteronomy is seen in the completeness of the invasion and the supposed extermination of the inhabitants. In Judges, it is seen in the way in which foreign oppression follows disloyalty to the God of Israel (this may be pre-Deuteronomic but it is in harmony with the Deuteronomic standpoint). In Samuel there is less trace of editorial standpoint; in Kings there is judgment given on the basis of the essential importance of centralized worship, and a connection is drawn between the religious attitude of the Kings and their prosperity and adversity. (There is also a Messianic tradition in Kings which makes much of the House of David—this is not found in Deuteronomy itself.) If at times we think that the Deuteronomic standpoint is formally and unilluminatingly applied to the history, we should remember that their fundamental conviction that the living God is the Lord of history is fundamentally right. And we must recognize that upon the traditions of the settlement in Palestine and of the Kingdoms of Israel and Judah is stamped the Deuteronomic conviction that to go with God is life, and to go against God is death.

## 4  Later Writings

In the later writings of the Old Testament the influence of Deuteronomy may be taken for granted. It has been found in particular in the prayer of Daniel (9.4-19); and the book of Job by its conscious revolt against the implications of Deuteronomic teaching bears witness to its great influence. The thought of Deuteronomy concerned primarily the prosperity and disaster of the nation, but even so, its teaching was too rigidly drawn and the problem of suffering given too narrow an answer. Job is no refutation of the main thesis of the Deuteronomist, but a vindication of the fact that the implications of the great choice for or against God are not to be seen immediately in all the happenings of life.

## 5   The Judaism of New Testament times
Upon the Judaism of New Testament times Deuteronomy stamped itself in great things and in little. The fundamental affirmation of the Jewish faith—the *Shema*<sup>c</sup> (which is recited morning and evening) is composed of two passages from this book, 6.4-9 and 9.13-21, supplemented by Num. 15.37-41, and the practice of thanksgiving after food received a warrant in 8.10. But in addition to these are the literal practices of the wearing of tassels (22.12), wearing phylacteries (6.8) and putting small cylinders containing the fundamentals of the faith on the doorposts of houses (6.9).

## 6   The New Testament
In the New Testament our Lord confesses his indebtedness to Deuteronomy by his reliance upon it in his temptation (6.13-16, 8.3, cp. Matt. 4.4, 7, 10, Luke 4.8, 12); he endorses its emphasis on the first and great commandment to ' love the Lord thy God with all thine heart, and with all thy soul and with all thy might' (6.5, cp. Matt. 22.37-38, Mark 12.29-33, Luke 10.27), and if the commandment like unto it is not found as a formula in Deuteronomy (but in Lev. 19.18) there are vivid and moving examples of what it means. It is possible also that our Lord found here in a limited application (18.13) the germ of the crucial thought in the Sermon on the Mount: be ye therefore perfect even as your heavenly Father is perfect (Matt. 5.48).

The apostle Paul makes a varied but not so searching a use of the book. He boldly applies its emphasis on the nearness of the covenant to the grace of Christ, and uses phrases from the Song of Moses to reinforce his arguments for the admission of the Gentiles, for whole-hearted loyalty to Christ, and for unwearied goodwill (30.12-14. cp. Rom. 10.6-8, 32.17-20. cp. Rom. 10.19, I Cor. 10.22, Rom. 12.19). He also weaves the Levitical curses and the curse for a hanged person into his argument for the Cross (27.26, 21.23, cp. Gal. 3.10, 13) and makes the unmuzzled ox serve as a reinforcement of his plea for the financial support of the ministry (Gal. 25.4, cp. I Cor. 9.9). In Hebrews there are echoes of the thunder of Horeb and a more literal application of the saying: Vengeance is mine (4.5, 32.35, cp. Heb. 12, 10.30). In Acts 3.22, 7.37 the promise of a prophet to speak God's word given in 18.15 is used as testimony to the meaning of the ministry of Jesus Christ.

This is a great book; and it has had a great influence. It speaks to us in the name of God across the centuries. We can leave aside its limitations as we read, and be nourished upon its great faith in God and man in the strength of which the Gospel of our Lord Jesus Christ came to claim man's soul for evermore.

*Commentary*

# PART ONE

## THE HISTORICAL SETTING
## OF THE COVENANT AND THE PREACHING
## OF ITS MEANING
## 1.1-11.32

### I

## THE FIRST SPEECH OF MOSES
### 1.1-4.49

### 1.1-5 Moses speaks to all Israel

The setting for the interpretation of the meaning of the Covenant of God with Israel is the land of Moab. The Deuteronomist is a preacher, not an historian, and he does not trace the movement of actual events. What he does is to interpret events from fixed points. These points are two: one is in Moab on the edge of the Promised Land, the other is the Mount of Horeb, where God has revealed himself as the God of Israel. In Moab, then, Moses speaks to all Israel, interpreting the way they have come, and giving further meaning of the revelation of God. The words in these verses seem definite, but are actually rather obscure, and come from different sources.

### 1.6-3.29 SURVEY OF ISRAEL'S JOURNEY
### FROM HOREB TO MOAB

### 1.6-46 *The Beginning of the Journey*

### 1.6-8 The start from Horeb

Deuteronomy is a reinterpretation of the tradition of Israel, and it presupposes a wider knowledge of that tradition. Here the revelation of God at Horeb is presupposed, and the journey of Israel is surveyed, not in detail, but at two points, the beginning and end of the journey. The meaning of the

journey is to be found in God's leading of his people into the
Promised Land. It is important to understand what is given
here is not meant to be present experience—the understanding
of events as they come one by one—but history, in the sense
of the understanding of events when the series has been completed and men can reflect on their meaning. Whatever people
felt at the time, it is this writer's conviction that it was by the
guidance of God that Israel made its journey and that the
land into which they came was given to them by God to fulfil
the promise made to their fathers.

## 1.9-18  The appointment of officers

The test of any movement comes when authority is delegated
from the leader to subordinates who can act in his place. Only
if the characteristic quality of the movement is exemplified in
lesser men as well as in the great is the power of the movement
being transmitted effectively. (The fact that the great leader
is available as here (v. 17) to bring his massive judgment and
experience to bear in difficult cases does not alter the real
delegation of responsibility.)

In this account of the delegation of judicial power by Moses
we have a statement of the meaning of justice which goes deep.
The men chosen are to be wise and understanding and known
—terms which imply not merely intellectual ability but moral
character and experience. They are to hear patiently and
judge impartially. They are not to RESPECT PERSONS, that is,
to give unfair advantage to the more important person. This
concern is emphasized throughout the Bible (cp. Ex. 23.3, Lev.
19.15, Ps. 82.2, Prov. 18.3, Mal. 2.9, II Chron. 19.7, Jas. 2.1-9,
Acts 10.34, Rom. 2.11, Eph. 6.9, Col. 3.25, I Pet. 1.17). The
judgment is God's, and therefore the judge must not be afraid
of man, but do God's will. The principle is far-reaching, whatever the limitations of early judicial procedure. There remains
still the problem that the judge should realize that his enuncia-
tion of God's judgment is limited and subject to error, and
that it needs modification in changed circumstances.

In v. 16 we have the first mention of the stranger or sojourner
(Hebrew gēr) who has such a large place in the concern of the

Deuteronomist, and associated with the fatherless and the widow as the objects of God's compassion and therefore of Israel's succour (cp. 10.19, 24.17, 27.19). The stranger means a non-Israelite who has come to live in Israel, and therefore normally dependent on the good treatment he receives from those who possess land. The duty of Israel to care for the stranger is the seed of the belief that faith in God means justice and mercy not only to the people of God but to any human being who needs it.

### 1.19-46   The fear of God and the fear of man

      19 From Horeb to Kadesh-Barnea
20-25 The Mission of the Spies
26-33 The disloyalty of the people
34-40 God's anger and judgments
41-46 Ineffective repentance

This section is an account of that sin of Israel, which, according to tradition, condemned it to wander forty years in the wilderness instead of going straight ahead to the promised land. The people rebel against the command of God to possess the land, because they are afraid: and then, when it is too late, they decide to go up and fight, though this is not now the will of God.

The story is true to the moral realities of life. People do behave like this. Leadership of a nation, or of a family or any other human grouping has to contend with similar human failings. We are reluctant to go forward with a difficult operation, even when we are committed to it and know that it is for our good. Much that we resent in our present experience is due to our previous failures. And often we attempt to make up for our moral failure to do the right thing at the right time by a light-hearted attempt to do now, at the wrong time, what we should have done before.

The variability of the word of God is true to the Biblical understanding of the living God. At one time God says GO UP AND POSSESS IT: FEAR NOT, NEITHER BE DISMAYED, at another time God says GO UP NOT, NEITHER FIGHT; FOR I AM NOT AMONG YOU; LEST YE BE SMITTEN BY YOUR ENEMIES. The word of God is always true to his unchanging purpose. It always calls for repentance, faith, obedience and love. But it is never stereotyped. Man cannot do the will of God by a blind acceptance of custom. There is no alternative to living moral obedience.

The passage suggests that the will of God was perfectly plain and definite to all concerned. But this is true to life only in retrospect. When the dust of controversy has settled, when the pressure of immediate decision is over, when subsequent events have made clear who was right and who was wrong, then the will of God may be seen as clearly as this passage shows. But at the time it was different. The difficulty of decision and the faults and failures of personalities get in the way of clear vision. Human leaders sometimes identify their plans and purposes too closely with the will of God. Resistance to those plans may not be, as they may imagine, rebellion against the commandment of God, but a legitimate difference of human judgment.

The Biblical record often takes for granted that problems of immediate human action have been met without concerning itself with them. It is important for us to realize that in our own experience of life things will not be quite as obvious as this passage suggests. A good illustration of this is given by the Old Testament itself. Compare the accounts of the conquest of Canaan in Joshua and Judges. In the former (written later) it is swift, clear-cut decisive: in the latter (nearer to the actual events) it is slow, painful and partial. We must not dismiss the reality of rebellion against the commandment of God given in this story, because the account of it does not reproduce all the confusion of actual life. Both rebellion against and obedience to the command of God are real experiences.

For Deuteronomy the judgment and blessing of God are immediate. Israel has witnessed the direct action of God in Egypt, and has seen how God has cared for Israel in the wilderness, shielding them from the hardships of the journey as a man would carry his son over a dark and difficult pathway. They cannot help knowing that to obey God will mean at once the overcoming of their enemies; and that to disobey God will mean at once God's punishment of their wickedness.

This theory of God's action won a great hold upon Israel, indeed it became the dominant theory of the Old Covenant, and great energies had to be expended in breaking its cramping bonds and seeking some more adequate understanding of the complexities of the relation between God and man. In spite of this, the Deuteronomic theory of immediate judgment and blessing from God still remains the theory popularly held with great tenacity by ordinary people. They may not believe that God does in fact act this way, but they expect him to do so if he is real.

For a living faith the theory is true—not false. It requires correction—substantial correction—but the fundamental idea remains essential to faith in the living God. There are a number of Einsteins to the Deuteronomic Newton, but they correct the application of the theory, not its fundamental truth. The judgment and blessing of God are none the less real because they are discerned by faith and are not immediately apparent to the materialistically-minded observer. The refusal of God's call does not have its effects wholly delayed beyond this present life. It may be all the more terrible because it works unseen for a long time before its dread effect becomes visible—like a deep-seated cancer with an insidious onset.

So, too, there is a blessing of God which is real. There is a difference between THE LORD YOUR GOD . . . SHALL FIGHT FOR YOU and I AM NOT AMONG YOU, AND SO YOU WILL BE SMITTEN BEFORE YOUR ENEMIES. The presence of God in the midst of his people can be recognized. From one point of view, the story of the Bible is the movement from expecting that presence to be seen primarily in military and political action, to seeing it as governing the ultimate springs of life. But for its presence there can be no substitute. The people of God cannot escape the need to give evidence that God is with them.

## 2.1-3.29  *The End of the Journey*

**2.1-23 The advance northwards from Mount Seir (cp. Num. 20)**
The Deuteronomist turns from the account of that sin which
kept Israel in the wilderness to the beginning of the journey
northwards which was to take them into the Promised Land.
The intervening years he dismisses briefly in v. 1 as MANY DAYS,
though we learn from v. 7 that the period was in round terms
'forty years' or more definitely from v. 14 that the time was
thirty-eight years.

In this interpretation of the tradition, Israel came into conflict neither with the people of Edom, nor with the people of
Moab, nor with the people of Ammon.  All these people
allowed a free passage and sold food and water.  The peasants
in the settled lands needed to guard their resources of food
and water against the incursions of large numbers of nomadic
people; on the other hand they found it profitable to sell
limited quantities of food and water to travellers through their
land.

There are differing interpretations in the Old Testament of
the meaning of the wilderness period.  Here, the emphasis is
upon God's care of his people.  Because God has been with
them—they have not wanted for anything.

The reason given for the refusal to disturb Edom, Moab
and Ammon, indicate that the God of Israel is acknowledged
to be something more than the God of Israel.  He has not only
given Israel its Promised Land, he has given to other peoples
their land as their possession.  In verses 10-12 and 20-23 we
have antiquarian notes, coming from a period long after the
settlement in Canaan, and telling of the legendary height and
strength of the original peoples who lived there.  Many ancient
peoples have this tradition of giants in bygone days.  For these
giants there are numerous names which do not add much to
our knowledge.

**2.24-37 Defeat of Sihon, King of Heshbon (cp. Num. 21.21-30)**
In this passage is the promise that God will begin to put the
fear of Israel and the dread of Israel upon the nations that are

under the whole heaven, who shall hear report of Israel and
shall tremble, and shall be in anguish because of Israel. This
may come from a nostalgic looking backward, from a time
when Israel was of no account as a fighting force, to a period
of military glory. The issue of power is raised unmistakably
here. The people of God have a dual citizenship, and if part
of this is in heaven, the other is on earth. If they do in fact
seek the extension of the reign of the living God, inevitably
they also seek the extension of the social influence of the
human group which worships God. We cannot ignore the
temporal power of the Church as part of the condition of
the existence of the Church.

Certain kinds of power are incompatible with obedience to
the will of God. Israel is portrayed here as having the
characteristics of a totalitarian power in exacting from other
nations abject submission and humiliation. That may have
been one of the strands in the basic tradition of Israel's history,
which in the mercy of God was transformed into the conception
of the suffering servant. There should remain for all possessors
of power, respect where it is deserved, trust where it is
awakened, and a concern that all men should act according to
their own informed conscience. Servile fear should never be
sought.

The passage tells us that Moses spoke WORDS OF PEACE.
This is not in all accounts, and may well spring from the
humanitarian concern shown by the Deuteronomist. Whatever the conflicts, physical or otherwise, into which we are
forced, it is in keeping with our faith—not to welcome conflict for its own sake, but to be glad when matters can be
arranged amicably without it.

We are also told that God hardened the spirit of Sihon,
king of Heshbon, that he might deliver him into Israel's hand.
Some scholars explain this by what they call the ' determinism '
of Hebrew thought, which sees the direct action of God in
everything. But the word ' determinism ' seems inapplicable,
because there is no minimizing of human responsibility. We
should interpret this feature of the Biblical record, as we have
its clear-cut character, in terms of how things seem in retro-

spect. Once Israel's conquests are taken for granted as opening the way into the Promised Land, then the obstinacy of Sihon can be seen as the inevitable doom of those who oppose God's purposes, and as part of the story which vindicates God's action.

The crucial and disturbing aspect of the story is this. AND WE TOOK ALL HIS CITIES AT THAT TIME, we read, AND UTTERLY DESTROYED THE MEN, THE WOMEN, AND THE LITTLE ONES OF EVERY CITY, WE LEFT NONE TO REMAIN: ONLY THE CATTLE WE TOOK FOR A PREY TO OURSELVES, AND THE SPOIL OF THE CITIES WHICH WE TOOK. This is an instance of the 'devotion' of the enemy to the Deity, and it arises from the fact that war is conceived as essentially a religious act. Both captives and spoil should be destroyed. In the Old Testament various attitudes are taken to this practice, and in particular we should note the conflict between Samuel and Saul (I Sam. 15) because Saul has spared the hated enemy king (see 25.17-19) and the best of the cattle. The conflict may be between the pure religious attitude which demands the dedication to the Deity of all enemy property by its destruction; and the semi-utilitarian attitude which is reluctant to destroy excellent property which could be put to advantageous use. Certainly this account attributes to Moses only a modified form of the 'ban', but even this includes the slaughtering of all men, women and children who belong to the enemy side.

We can say, to begin with, that much of the account of slaughtering in the Old Testament is due to the bloodthirsty imagination of pious people remote from the happenings of war, and not to the actual practice of those who did the fighting (compare, again, the more historical account of Judges with the later account of Joshua). If Israel's wars had exterminated the opposing population to the extent recorded, some of the persistent problems of Israel in the promised land would have been eliminated.

Yet in God's world many terrible and beastly things happen, and we must understand his will in relation to experiences that befall men and women. And we are here presented with a cruel and inhuman act as part of the way of life of the

people of God. The conquest of Canaan is not a side-issue:
it is essential to the inheritance of the promised land.

What is the place of war in God's universe? War has been
an instrument of change—perhaps the major instrument of
change in the world. And a dispassionate analysis must
admit that some of the changes brought about by war have
been for good. Has war ever been the instrument of God's
purpose? We must say that war has never been used by God
for setting out his Gospel of redemption. War is not God's
positive purpose for his world. And yet we must admit that
war is associated with the redemption from Egypt. We may
say that the actual Exodus was the passive action of with-
drawal, and that all militaristic action was on the side of the
Egyptians. Yet we cannot wholly separate the Exodus from
the settlement in Canaan, and however limited the infiltration
may have been, we cannot wholly dissociate it from fighting.
We must, however, maintain that the deliverance is the essential thing—not the conquest.

If war has been used of God, it has been as indicating a
concern for moral purpose against a materialistic view of
life. We must not be cynical too easily here, lest by our
cynicism we deny a real touch of God upon our human life.
Beyond all this there is the truth embodied in the words
' Surely the wrath of man shall praise Thee ' (Ps. 76.10).
Even things which are intrinsically evil are used in mysterious
ways by God to further his gracious purpose.

The impact of war is very different in the New Testament
from what it is in the Old. This is partly due to the fact that
we have moved from a national to a universalist and personal
setting. There is still conflict between good and evil, in which
we must endure hardness: but it is not a military conflict. We
have moved to a new depth of the grace of God which reaches
deeper than the fate of nations. But there still remains
the problem of relating the grace and mercy of God in Christ
to the problems of national existence, and these involve not
merely moral and social power, but in the end, physical
force.

### 3.1-7 Defeat of Og, King of Bashan (cp. Num. 21.31-35)

The defeat of Og, King of Bashan, is the same type of incident as that which has just been recounted. Sihon and Og were linked in the public memory of Israel and were celebrated in later song (cf. Ps. 135.11, 136.20) probably as the last serious obstacles to the fulfilment of the promise of the Exodus, and the entry of the Israelites into the Promised Land.

No appeal is made to Og for permission to pass through his land. This may be due in the mind of the Deuteronomist to the fact that some people show their character so plainly in advance that we know that appeals which we might make to others would be unavailing; it might also be due to the fact that the defeat of Sihon made fighting inevitable.

Og, we learn from v. 11, was a giant: and the conquest of this gigantic enemy in the name of Yahweh the God of Israel may have had a symbolic value for Israel over and beyond the result of the victory won.

### 3.8-20 Assignment of Conquered Territory (Num. 32)

It is part of the tradition of Israel that the lands east of the Jordan were allotted to the tribes of Reuben, and Gad, and the half-tribe of Manasseh. The women and children were left in the settlements with the accumulated wealth, and the men accompanied their fellows to assist in the entrance into the Promised Land.

In v. 9 we have an antiquarian note about Mount Hermon. Sirion (Ps. 29.6) and Senir (Ezek. 27.5, S. Songs 4.8, I Chron. 5.23) may be different names for parts of the long mountain.

v. 11 is a famous antiquarian note. It was obviously written much later than the time of Moses, and was one of the factors which pointed the way to the historical analysis of the books of the Old Testament. In Rabbah there was a survival from ancient days—a sarcophagus of black basalt, called in our version A BEDSTEAD OF IRON. If we take the cubit as about eighteen inches the sarcophagus was thirteen and a half feet by six. (This is the ordinary cubit, which was originally the length of the lower arm: later we find a larger cubit (Ezek. 40.5; 43.13).)

v. 14 is an insertion based on Num. 32.41.

### 3.21-22   The Command to Joshua

This command to Joshua at this time is not recorded elsewhere in the Pentateuch. It follows the pattern of Biblical
faith. First there is experience of God's action. Then,
arising out of that experience, a different kind of conduct.
The events in which God's action is seen vary considerably,
and the resulting action is correspondingly different. But this
is the basis of all Biblical testimony to the impact of God
upon the lives of men.

### 3.23-29   The prayer of Moses and its rejection (cp. Num. 27.12-23)

That Moses died before reaching the Promised Land is taken
for granted in all the traditions of Israel. Why did not Moses
enter the Promised Land? We have two explanations given
in the Old Testament. One given here (cp. 1.38) is that God
was angry with Moses on account of the sin of the people
from which Moses himself had tried to dissuade them. The
other, given in Num. 27.12-14, is also the basis of the account
in 32.48-52. It finds the reason in Moses striking the rock
for the water to flow at Kadesh (Num. 20.2-29). In this
latter account (see 32.49) the mountain which Moses is
told to climb is called 'Nebo' whereas here it is called
'Pisgah'.

George Adam Smith comments on the verse O LORD, THOU
HAST BEGUN TO SHOW THY SERVANT THY GREATNESS by saying:
'But not fulfilled in my sight!' A pathetic emphasis. Moses
prayed to see with his own eyes the completion of the great
Providence carried so far at his hands. This temper is characteristic of all Deuteronomy: the passion to experience the full-
rounded Providence of God in this life, absolutely no hope of
another! As time went on a nobler trust was born. The
servant of Jehovah 'cut off from the land of the living', yet
'sees of the travail of his soul and is satisfied' (Isa. 53.11)
and Jesus 'becoming obedient even unto death' (Phil. 2.8),
'for the joy set before him endured the cross, despising the

shame' (Heb. 12.2) 'Let this cup pass from me . . . never-
theless . . . thy will be done.

This is movingly and illuminatingly said, but it is in part
unfair. Even granted the deeper faith in the eternal Kingdom
of God, it is natural to want to see here on earth at least the
fulfilment of some part of the work which we have been
doing in the name of God. That Moses did not live to see
the completion of his leadership of his people in the actual
entrance to the Promised Land, seemed to Israel a mystery,
which needed explanation, and we may acknowledge the mystery too. But life on earth, even for the greatest, is no rounded
whole; and the important thing is that Moses had done the
work that God had entrusted to him.

The tradition that Moses was prevented from going over
into the Promised Land because of the sin of the people ought
to be associated with the precious tradition of vicarious suffering in the Bible (cp. 9.15-20, 25-29 and Ex. 32.31-32). It is
true that this association in sin is not voluntarily accepted by
Moses but demanded by God, but it points to something
precious. As we think of Moses who brought his people to
the Promised Land, but could not himself enter, we are
reminded of him of whom it was said (Mark 15.31) 'He
saved others; himself he cannot save'; and of the apostle who
said (Rom. 9.3) 'I could wish that myself were accursed from
Christ for my brethren, my kinsmen according to the flesh.'

### 4.1-40 Moses appeals to Israel to obey the Law, because of the greatness of the revelation of God at Horeb

This is a great passage of religious exhortation. It may be
summed up as follows:

    1-8   Keep the Law
    9-24  Do not worship idols
    25-31 Remember the judgment and mercy of God
    32-40 Remember the greatness of God

**2. Ye shall not add to the word which I command you,
neither shall ye diminish ought from it.** The positive message
is well expressed by Joseph Parker: 'You must not fit the
word to you, you must fit yourselves to the word.' Israel

must not betray by any additions and subtractions that assurance to which Deuteronomy witnesses that there is one God of grace who demands righteousness of all men. But the words can also be taken in a narrow legalist temper, as they have been in history; and, then, obedience to God is prescribed for us in meticulous detail, and means only resigned compliance. The word of God in both Old Covenant and New is at once both final and not to be superseded; and also capable of provoking new creative interpretations and fashionings of experience.

**3. Baal Peor** has not previously been mentioned; it belongs to that wider tradition, knowledge of which the Deuteronomist presupposes. We can read about it in Num. 25.1-5 where the Israelites who have intermarried with the Moabites and worshipped the Baal of Peor were all killed to a man. This is history idealized, or, in other terms, history sharpened to an intolerable sense of the immediate judgment of God upon sin. Here the urgency of the preacher's emphasis on the need to turn away from sin has infected the narrative.

**6.** Because of the New Testament, we have a keen sense of the limitations of the Law: we must also have a sense of its greatness. Prophecy and Law belong together, for the Law is, in part at least, the application of prophetic teaching to life; its injunctions are all marked by the influence of prophecy. The impress of the Law upon Israel gave them as a people a moral integrity and a humanity that lifted them above other nations and made foreigners anxious to learn the secret of their life. So the Deuteronomist says that for Israel God is near, and their statutes are righteous. We, too, must say this. To affirm the centrality for all men of God's revelation in Christ means that he is near to us in the press of daily living; we can only meet the chaotic uncertainty of to-day by affirming that the standards which arise from faith in Christ are fair, and upright, and utterly reliable.

In v. 13 occurs the first instance in this book of the word *berith*, covenant, which is so fundamental for the understanding of the faith of Israel. It is important not to think of the covenant as a legal arrangement or as a bargain. It does not mean that God would look after Israel so long as Israel was faithful, nor that Israel would obey God so long as he brought prosperity to them. The Covenant is founded on the deliverance of Israel which God has already brought about. God has loved Israel and chosen them to be his people. In the Covenant God claims Israel as his own people, and through their acceptance of it seeks to bring them into true relation with himself. In accepting the Covenant Israel promises to be loyal to God and to live in a manner worthy of the great privilege of being God's people (see chap. 5 and 26.16-19).

In the section to which this verse belongs (vv. 9-24), Israel is warned against idolatry in view of the great events at Horeb. We ought to be aware in reading this passage that the writer to the Hebrews has it in mind when, in chapter 12, he contrasts with the revelation at Horeb, the revelation in the heavenly Jerusalem, the general assembly and church of the first-born, and Jesus, the mediator of the New Covenant, and the blood of sprinkling that speaketh better things than that of Abel. In spite of the contrast, the writer links up with Deuteronomy in affirming that God is a consuming fire.

**10.** Israel is exhorted to remember THE DAY THAT THOU STOODEST BEFORE THE LORD THY GOD IN HOREB. Whether it is due to the mingling of different traditions or not, we must note that sometimes Deuteronomy lays stress on the passing away of the original generation, and sometimes it insists that the present Israel has seen and remembered all that happened at Horeb. This latter has the profoundest religious meaning. Each succeeding generation of God's people is contemporary with the events of revelation.[1] The idea is expressed vividly in the negro spiritual: ' Were you there when they crucified my Lord? ' Yes, we were there. Our eyes have seen. The great events of God's revelation have become immediately present to us.

We should note the Deuteronomic understanding of Horeb. (For practical purposes the names Horeb and Sinai used in different traditions of Israel are interchangeable in meaning.) We may be able to penetrate behind this tradition to a nearer

[1] cp. W. D. Davies: *Paul and Rabbinic Judaism*, pp. 102ff.

view of history, but we must begin by understanding the
tradition. It is a tradition of a mountain burning with fire,
surrounded by darkness, clouds, and thick darkness, and
Yahweh the God of Israel speaking out of the midst of the
fire. Israel hears the words, but sees no form.

This intense conviction of the invisible moral reality of
God has been the power enabling Israel to break free from
worshipping natural powers as God. It was a tremendous
struggle to achieve this victory and Israel must remember it.
Perhaps Protestantism, laying hold of this Deuteronomic word,
has stressed too much the necessity of abandoning visible
symbols, as it emphasized the positive worth of audible symbols as a means of maintaining fellowship with God. But the
human mind has a persistent tendency to content itself with
substitutes for the living God. The victory of God over idols
of wood and stone and over the natural forces of the universe
was a great achievement in the history of mankind. Though
men fell back into superstitious practices we may hope that it
is a victory won once for all.

But the winning of this victory has only given the struggle a
more interior form. Our idolatry has become refined. We
worship aspects of life—we put our own desires in the place of
God. And the struggle against idolatry takes place not only
in the world, but in the Church. God's call to men is not to be
content so easily with these stultifying and frustrating allegiances, but to storm the Kingdom of God and to be content
with nothing less than the life of God himself.

vv. 25-31 insist that idolatry will produce destruction and
exile, but that if from exile Israel turns to God in penitence,
he will be found and remember his Covenant. Perhaps this
passage was written after the historical experience of exile.
The main fact for us is the possibility it offers of repentance and
renewal from God. The God of the Old Covenant is a God of
mercy. The eternal life which he offers can only be had on
his terms, but he always offers the renewal of life.

When we read the story of the Prodigal Son we must not
think of it as saying something unheard of in Israel's history.
It sharpens and brings into vivid focus that offer of renewal

to the penitent which sounds out from the Old Covenant. If, in the far country, Israel repents, there is a welcome waiting from God. This message is not at all outmoded to-day. We must offer to those who are astray from God, and uncertain of his presence, the certainty that God is anxious to reveal himself to the seeking soul. God can be found in this day of uncertainty, and we have warrant for saying so.

Here, as elsewhere, we have the mention of other gods beside the God of Israel. We have to acknowledge that the understanding of Israel's faith has not yet come to the full acknowledgement of the one true God. But this is no obstacle to the Christian reader. He can notice the historical limitation, but recognize that even so, the passage witnesses to the claim of the living God and has in it the promise and power of serving as the channel for the revelation of Jesus Christ our Lord.

vv. 32-40 exhort Israel to remember the greatness of God. Has there ever been a revelation of God such as Israel has had—God speaking out of the midst of the fire, and delivering Israel from Egypt with TEMPTATIONS, SIGNS, WONDERS, WARS, AND GREAT TERRORS? God has revealed himself to Israel that Israel might know him and he has done this out of his love and choice. Since, then, Israel knows the true God of heaven and earth, Israel must keep his laws and find in obedience the fulness of life on earth.

Here the language of oratory in the service of religious truth rises to its height. The details that are adduced of the revelation at Horeb may or may not impress us; but it is to be hoped that our response to the question is as affirmative as the preacher means it to be. Some of the reasons traditionally given for the superiority of the Mosaic revelation (e.g. its greater antiquity than any other) have gone; but in the intimacy and truth of its revelation of the living God, and, in spite of its limitations, the magnificence of its stress on righteousness of life, this revelation of God surpasses all others until it is surpassed by the New Covenant.

We, who have lived under loyalty to Christ, minimize that loyalty if we do not thrill to the claim of allegiance to God

made known in the Old Covenant. This is the true God and
there is none else. In our response we draw near to him,
who, in his eternal love, elected Israel to be the means of
proclaiming that love to all men. And the election of Israel
is fulfilled in the greater glory of God's election of his eternal
Son—not to annul the Old Covenant, but to bring its purposes
more surely to pass. Horeb and Calvary, two points in
human history—the one surpassing the other—belong together
in their inexhaustible resources for rekindling the life of man
in the faith of the one true God.

### 4.41-43  Three Cities of Refuge
The Deuteronomic law on cities of refuge is given in 14.1-13.
There we read of cities west of the Jordan, but not of any
cities east of it. There is a later tradition given more elabor-
ately in Num. 35.9-34 in which six cities are named, three on
either side of the Jordan. In Josh. 20 the six cities on either
side of the Jordan are appointed by Joshua—these include
the cities east of the Jordan, Bezer, Ramoth, and Golan—
said here to have been appointed by Moses. We can treat
this passage only as a late insertion by someone who did not
know the tradition that Joshua had appointed these cities.
On the purpose and value of cities of refuge see 19.1-13.

### 4.44-49  Introduction to the giving of the Law in Moab
This passage constitutes one of the difficulties of knowing just
where the book of Deuteronomy originally began. It is not a
continuation of what has gone before: it is an alternative to
it. Perhaps v 44 was the beginning and the other verses are a
summary of the material given in 1.1-4.40. As the material
is all Deuteronomic, we have no real certainty in the matter.

# II

## THE SECOND SPEECH OF MOSES
### 5.1-11.32

### 5.1-21 The Covenant of God with Israel at Horeb

In chap. 5 we turn back from Moab to remember the Revelation of God at Horeb. Deuteronomy has a very clear idea as to what happened at Horeb, and gives to that event a uniqueness which is not ascribed to the subsequent legislation.

In vv. 1-5 we are told that THE COVENANT (see notes on 4.13 and 26.16-19) was not made WITH OUR FATHERS BUT WITH US WHO ARE HERE ALIVE. This is in formal contradiction with the statements about the generation that has perished, but it is religiously right. The covenant of God is made with past, present, and future generations. The essential thing is that we share in it at first hand and not at second hand. v. 5 is to be taken as an interpolation, as a not very intelligent reconciliation of these opening verses with the end of the chapter. The passage really insists that the Decalogue has a divine authority above all subsequent legislation, and that this was heard by all Israel. The lines are drawn very sharply in Deuteronomy, in contrast with Exodus (cp. Ex. 19.14-19; 20.18-21) where it is not clear whether the people heard anything definite at all.

At Horeb God made a covenant with Israel. The content of that covenant so far as the fundamental obligations of Israel are concerned consists in the ' Ten Words ' given in vv. 6-21. The more familiar form is that found in Ex. 20.1-17. The Deuteronomic version is certainly more elaborate than that given in Exodus, though they may profitably be regarded as parallel rather than antithetic.

Can either of them be ascribed to Moses? In Ex. 34.14-26 Israel is given a decalogue, which has, as its distinctive feature, ritual rather than ethical requirement; and some scholars have seen in this the original Mosaic tradition. But it is more

49

D

likely to come from the tradition of Israel which had not felt
the impact of the transformation which Moses gave.
H. H. Rowley says:[1] 'To find in the Ethical Decalogue, in its
original unexpanded form, the hand of Moses, is not to find
here some isolated phenomenon, unrelated to all else we know
of Moses, and unrelated to the rest of his work, but to find
something that belongs naturally to it. The transition from
a primitive decalogue of the type of the Ritual Decalogue to
the Ethical Decalogue was not one that would happen by
itself with the lapse of time. It was brought about by some
dynamic personality, and on every ground the tradition that
connects the higher decalogue with Moses is to be credited.'

The main obstacle which scholars have found to ascribing
the decalogue to Moses is the prohibition of the making of
images. It is to be noted that the account in Num. 21.4-9 of
the bronze serpent which Moses made is not to be attributed
to Moses himself, but is a story told to explain a symbol
whose origin lay outside the tradition of Yahweh as the God
of Israel; and in any case there is no evidence that it was
intended to be an image of Yahweh. It is, of course, true
that images were used long after the time of Moses (cp. Judg.
17.1-6, I Sam. 19.13-16), but there is no evidence that an
image of Yahweh was made before the time of Jeroboam I,
and then the image which he chose was a Canaanite one.
The ritual decalogue itself prohibits images though the ones
mentioned are molten (graven images being prohibited in
Deut. 5 and Ex. 20) and it seems probable that the faith in
Yahweh the God of Israel was always imageless.

What is clear is that the witness of Moses to the meaning
of Yahweh the God of Israel had initially a smaller acceptance
in Israel than later tradition suggests; but there is growing
agreement that the fundamental conviction of the decalogue
that the worship of God and the practice of moral living belong
together, comes from Moses himself. In principle the work
of the eighth-century prophets is a vindication of the work of
Moses—surpassing it and giving it new vitality, but not super-
seding it.

[1] *The Re-Discovery of the Old Testament*, p. 87.

However that may be, for the Deuteronomist, the Decalogue is the content of the Mosaic covenant; and whatever its historical origin, we must do justice to its permanent worth. Great religious communities have differed in opinion as to the way it should be split into ten parts as follows:

|  | Greek and Reformed | Roman Catholic and Lutheran | Jewish |
|---|---|---|---|
| God the deliverer out of Egypt | Preface | Preface | 1st |
| Prohibition of polytheism | 1st | 1st | 2nd |
| Prohibition of graven images | 2nd | 1st | 2nd |
| From wrong use of divine Name to false witness | 2nd to 9th | 2nd to 8th | 3rd to 9th |
| Prohibition of covetousness | 10th | 9th and 10th | 10th |

George Adam Smith gives the following as the chief Christian expositions of the theological contents of the Decalogue. From the Roman side, Catechism of the Council of Trent, Part iii, chaps. 1-10. From the Protestant, the *Larger Westminster Catechism*, John Forbes ('the Aberdeen Doctor') *Theologia Moralis*, and R. W. Dale, *The Ten Commandments*. See also Prof. W. P. Paterson's article 'The Decalogue' in Hastings *Dictionary of the Bible*.

The Decalogue begins in v. 6 with the affirmation of the delivering power of the God of Israel. If we want to find the content of the covenant, here it is. Yahweh the God of Israel, who has delivered Israel from Egypt, covenants with Israel to be their God. The reality of that covenant on God's part is something that Israel only dimly understands. The limitations which Israel puts on God's meaning will only be overcome through disappointment and struggle. But men can escape from the limitations which they themselves set upon God's purposes into that larger vision to which he constrains them. God's commitment to humanity is always greater than we admit, because we are unworthy of and unready for its truth and power.

In Biblical faith, in the Old Testament as well as in the New, the Saviourhood of God is the key to our understanding of him as Creator or Judge. Whatever the demands of the covenant may be, they presuppose the experience of God's deliverance. The religion of the Old Covenant is primarily a religion of grace. 'The law was given by Moses, but grace and truth came by Jesus Christ' (John 1.17) is too harsh a judgment born out of the revolutionary Christian upheaval to stand as absolute truth. There is indeed a contrast, but it must be expressed differently. The New Testament is a witness to a greater redemption, but the redemptive character of the Old Covenant is fundamental.

It is natural to think of the Decalogue in terms of love to God and love to man, but it seems better to put the fifth commandment in the first table and accept the division into laws of piety and probity. The first law of piety in v. 7 calls for the recognition that Yahweh, the God of Israel, is one and the same God wherever he is worshipped. He has the same character wherever men call upon him. And it calls for that exclusive allegiance to the one true God of Israel which is the passionate plea of the whole Book of Deuteronomy. No doubt the word is not strictly monotheistic, in that it may presuppose the existence of other gods. But it gains instead of losing from this, because the fact that there is only one true God does not mean that people cannot choose. The 'gods' that gain the allegiance of men and women may be quite unreal compared with the living God, but they hold them none the less. The first commandment is the affirmation that our final loyalty must be given to the living God and to nothing else.

The second commandment prohibits the making of images, and is an affirmation of the Mosaic conviction of the moral reality of God, which was reinforced by the struggle of the eighth-century prophets against the worship of natural forces. God is not a material object and is not to be treated as such. This commandment is a real factor in turning men's minds from unworthy thoughts of God to the sublimity of him who is creator of heaven and earth. Once the nature of the true God can be taken for granted, something of the rigour of this commandment can be lessened. Differing attitudes have been taken in Christian history to the use of physical symbols in Christian worship. The answer seems to be that physical symbols are allowable, and even desirable, provided they do not in any way endanger the central conviction of the Old Covenant that God is above and beyond all material objects.

In vv. 9-10 we have an insistence on the exclusive claims of God and the persisting results of obedience and disobedience to him. The word JEALOUS with us often means unreasonably suspicious, but there is nothing of that meaning here. Instead, it means that claim for utterly exclusive loyalty which is alone worthy of God. The metaphor of marriage, prominent especially in Hosea and Jeremiah, expresses a relationship in which intimacy and fidelity are indispensable. That there are consequences of spiritual allegiance for good and evil, to the third and fourth generation, is a condition of human existence.

God's visitation of iniquity to the third and fourth generations is the result of human actions working themselves out, and not a witness to his intention. However true it may be that in Deuteronomy God's hatred is as real as his love, the distinction between what God allows and what God deliberately does though not yet explicit, is moving towards expression. This visitation of iniquity on later generations is not part of that action of God which is to be imitated: for human punishment must be limited to the man himself (see 24.16, cp. Jer. 31.29-30, Ezek. 18.1-4). The truth of the solidarity of the generations in good and evil must be balanced by the truth that every man must suffer for his own sins. The word

translated 'mercy' in the A.V.—Hebrew *hesed*—is one of
the great words of the Bible. It implies utterly faithful
devotion, and unites both affection and loyalty. God will
never desert those who trust in him.

Whatever the particular sin at which the third commandment was originally aimed, perhaps some form of false
swearing or magical incantation, it warns us to treat the
name of God with full reverence. There is a persistent danger
of our degrading God to a means to further our own purposes,
and we need to be recalled constantly to the fact that God is
he upon whom we depend, whose Name is holy, the most
stupendous fact of all life. The positive affirmation of which
this is the negative counterpart, is given in the Lord's
Prayer.

The fourth commandment, to keep the Sabbath, is given
in vv. 12-15. The seventh day is to be kept holy for God.
The motive for the acknowledgement of the Sabbath is that
men and women should have rest, and is given twice over.
THAT THY MANSERVANT AND THY MAIDSERVANT MAY REST AS
WELL AS THOU states the humane concern, the remembrance
of Israel's deliverance from slavery in Egypt states the ground
on which permanent appeal is mad⸍ for generosity to the
weak. The reason given in Ex. 20.11, which is probably
later than our version here, also appeals to God's action,
but to his rest after the labours of creation. These reasons
may be regarded as supplementary theological motives for
the acknowledgement of the Sabbath, containing the double
concern for rest and worship. Christians do not acknowledge
the Jewish Sabbath, but admit the requirements in the Decalogue in its broad claim and blessing. The day Christians
acknowledge is the day of the Lord's Resurrection, and that
is a greater act of God to be honoured in the one day of the
week set apart for him than either of those mentioned in
Exodus or Deuteronomy. It is called the Lord's Day in
Rev. 1.10, and its use by Christians is mentioned in the New
Testament (Acts 20.7 and I Cor. 16.2). The detailed use of
one day as a day of worship and rest is, of course, not given
in the Decalogue, and rests on tradition and custom. But

it is important to observe that the requirement of the Decalogue as distinct from Jewish practice in the first century is
acknowledged and not repudiated by Christians in their
celebration of the day of the Lord's Resurrection.

We may add to the first table, the fifth commandment to
honour parents. The family and the worship of God belong
together, and the acknowledgement of family affections and
obligations is part of the way to God. The commandment
is called by St. Paul 'the first commandment with promise'
(Eph. 6.2-3). The promise is found in both versions, and it
is true that the stability of a nation is the stability of its
families. The disruption of the family is the surest way to
national decadence. In the New Testament we have in the
ministry of Jesus both an insistence that the obligations to
parents must be loyally kept (Matt. 15.3-6), the recognition
of a greater loyalty to wife (Matt. 19.5) and the insistence that
the Kingdom of God takes precedence of family loyalties
(Luke 14.26). Even the honouring of parents can be misused
if it is not brought under the over-riding claims of God, and
if it is treated as an opportunity of tyranny. But respect and
affection towards parents has a kinship with respect and
affection for God.

The second table of the Decalogue, commandments of
probity, are much less elaborated. Comment has been made
that these precepts are very elementary, and do not touch
the higher realms of human conduct. This is true, but as
we cannot take for granted the observance of the elementary
rules of conduct we had better begin here and worry about
the superstructure afterwards. v. 13. Killing is the ultimate
act of breach of fellowship with a brother man. All such
breaches of fellowship are contrary to the will of God. v. 14
The sacredness of the marriage bond is essential to true
human life. v. 15. Where dishonesty is rife no one benefits.
The prophets steadily denounced dishonesty, and the incul-
cation of honesty is one of the characteristic features of
Biblical faith. v. 16. The basis of true community is mutual
trust. Lying, like theft, cuts at the root of trust between
man and man. v. 21. The Deuteronomic form of the tenth

commandment puts the wife first, uses two different verbs, and adds the word 'field'. The double verb has led to this being treated as two commandments in Roman Catholic and Lutheran tradition. The commandment probably originally meant: do not lay hands on your neighbour's property. St. Paul's use of the term covet in Rom. 7.7, while not out of keeping with Deuteronomic law, is probably a development of the original meaning. The commandment is interpreted in Mark 10.19 as 'defraud not'.

The Decalogue has been treated as an expression of the 'natural law' governing all men. This is a conception which could only have arisen in a civilization dominated by the Christian Church. The justification for it is that at least the precepts of the second table are widely held throughout the world; and that, where the Christian faith could be taken for granted, or where it confronted only alternative faiths markedly similar in some respects, e.g. Judaism and Islam, the little amount of institutional requirement would hardly be noticed, and its concentration on the fundamental relation between God and man would seem its sole characteristic. The Decalogue does, indeed, according to Deuteronomy, give the fundamental requirement of God from man, a requirement of which the rest of the laws of the Pentateuch are only an elaboration. But it is a requirement in the setting of the covenant of God with Israel, and deriving its justification from that.

The Decalogue, in either its Exodic or Deuteronomic form, is taken seriously in the New Testament. It may be noted that when quoted, the order of the commandments is not always the same (cp. Matt. 19.18-19, Rom. 13.9, Luke 18.20). (However, the Septuagint Codex B has the New Testament order, and this also is given in the Nash Papyrus in Hebrew.)

One aspect of our Lord's attitude to the Decalogue consists in that summary of the Law which he either made himself or accepted from one of his hearers (Mark 12.28-34; Luke 10.25-28): Thou shalt love the Lord thy God with all thy heart, and with all thy soul, and with all thy strength, and with all thy mind; and thy neighbour as thyself. But more important still is the teaching of the Sermon on the Mount in which, while the commandments are left standing, they are pushed to their utmost possibility of meaning—the prohibition of killing becomes the prohibition of anger (Matt. 5.21-24), the prohibition of adultery becomes the prohibition of the lustful look (Matt. 5.27-28). This teaching of Jesus does not abolish the ten commandments, it takes them seriously. Only when they are taken seriously can we press on to the higher possibilities of the Kingdom. The apostle Paul here, as elsewhere, follows his master. His interpretation of the tenth commandment in Rom. 7.7 is not the literal meaning, but the farthest limit of spiritual fulfilment. We may also note that he understood love to neighbour as epitomizing the second table of law (Rom. 13.8-10).

### 5.22-33  The reception of the Covenant at Horeb

The remainder of the chapter describes the reception of the Covenant at Horeb, and the promise of the people to obey the commandments which Moses shall speak in God's name and which he is now (according to Deuteronomy) giving in Moab. This account of Horeb is continued later in the historical illustration given in 9.8-10.11.

Here God gives the law, and it is made quite clear from the words AND HE ADDED NO MORE that the Decalogue has a unique divine authority. This is heightened by the statement that God wrote them on TWO TABLES OF STONE. This cannot come from a period in which there were actually two tables of stone believed written by God himself, as these would have acted precisely as a magical God-substitute against which it is one of the purposes of Deuteronomy to battle. We must take the phrase as symbolizing their divine origin.

A third factor emphasizes the special character of the Decalogue. According to Deuteronomy, the people hear God speak the Decalogue and this alone; they plead that they cannot bear any more, and ask Moses to listen on their behalf, and say that they will do all that God says. It is not clear whether in the account in Ex. 19-21 the people heard anything from God directly. They certainly asked Moses to

listen on their behalf. In Deuteronomy alone is God's approval
mentioned.

In v. 29 God wishes that they might always be in this frame
of mind. Deuteronomy represents Horeb as the true norm of
Israel's life to which Israel must return. This is a characteristic moment in the life of faith. Thus the poet William
Cowper sang:

> Where is the blessedness I knew
> When first I saw the Lord?
> Where is the soul-refreshing view
> Of Jesus and His Word?

And the apostle Paul exposes the source of his own missionary
activity in the words 'I was not disobedient to the heavenly
vision' (Acts 26.19).

In vv. 30-31 God promises to reveal to Moses that way of
obedience which is the way of life and prosperity. It is the
way of obedience which Moses is represented as communi-
cating to the people at Moab.

The crucial verse of the section is v. 27: GO THOU NEAR AND
HEAR ALL THAT THE LORD OUR GOD SHALL SAY: AND SPEAK
THOU UNTO US. The problem of mediation remains with us.
We may rightly think that we have in Christ a nearer relation
with God than this secondary relation which is accorded the
people of Israel. But we are not freed from the necessity of
having this relation mediated to us.

Many have seen in Jeremiah's prophecy of a new covenant
(31.31-34) something which has already been fulfilled in
Christ. Professor T. H. Robinson wrote of this prophecy:[2]
'The old covenant had been shattered, but a new one would
be offered in its place. And this time the weakness of the old
would be avoided. It had failed, as Jeremiah saw, because it
had been an external thing, written down in a book and imposed on men by royal or ecclesiastical authority. Not so
can the dealings of man with God be rightly ordered. The
only authority which is valid in the last resort is that which

[2] *Prophecy and the Prophets*, 1923, p. 141.

comes from within. The only authority which can carry its
own fulfilment is that which has a man's personality behind it,
which grips his very soul and carries him forward by its own
momentum. There is no alteration in the terms, " I will become
their God and they shall become my people." But the method
of its establishment is to be changed. Deuteronomy with all
its magnificent ideals, was nothing but a " scrap of paper ";
the New Covenant would work, because it was to be written
on men's hearts.'

But it must be recognized that the New Covenant written
on men's hearts is not yet here, even in the Gospel of Christ,
and that it needs for its fulfilment the victory of God's everlasting Kingdom. As Wheeler Robinson says:[3] 'So long as
the ideal of Jeremiah awaits fulfilment, and the law of God
remains unwritten on the heart, some external authority in
religion, Bible or Church, will be necessary to correct the
vagaries of the individual, and to develop the possibilities of
the immature.'

### The Covenant at Moab: a Commentary on the First Commandment

### 6.1-11.32

The next six chapters give the meaning of the Old Covenant
as Deuteronomy understands it. That is: love and obedience
to the one true God of Israel. The meaning of this exclusive
loyalty these chapters reiterate again and again in language of
passionate exhortation.

#### 6.1-25  Love and Obedience are due to the one true God

|       |                                      |
|-------|--------------------------------------|
| 1-3   | Obedience will bring prosperity      |
| 4-9   | The fundamental faith and duty       |
| 10-15 | Beware of forgetting God             |
| 16-19 | Do not put God to the test, but obey |
| 20-25 | The meaning of law is redemption     |

The chapter opens with an affirmation of the Deuteronomic

[3] *Century Bible*, p. 44.

conviction that obedience to God is the source of well-being. In Israel's continued faithfulness lies her continuing prosperity.

4-9 form the first paragraph of the Jewish *Shema*<sup>c</sup> (=Hear), completed by 11.13-21 and Num. 15.37-41. It is the first scripture taught to Jewish children and is set to be recited by every Jew morning and evening. It is a noble confession of faith in the one God and of response to him.

The phrase THE LORD OUR GOD IS ONE LORD is elliptical in the Hebrew and has three other possible renderings: 'The Lord our God, the Lord is one', or 'the Lord is our God, the Lord is one', or 'the Lord is our God, the Lord alone'. The phrase is not formally monotheistic (cp. I Cor. 8.4-6), but it is a quite explicit affirmation of the sole allegiance of Israel. To this one God is to be given the complete affection of his worshippers. As Matthew Henry says, 'we are to love God with a sincere love, a strong love, a superlative love, an intelligent love, an entire love'. And this commandment is accepted by Jesus as the great commandment (Mark 12.29; Matt. 22.37; Luke 10.27-28).

The uniting of love and obedience to God is of the greatest importance for the life of faith. This is the fruit of the teaching of the prophets Amos and Hosea, fully and freely accepted. Adam Welch expounds this chapter under the title 'He is a Jew which is one inwardly' (cp. Rom. 2.29), and that expresses the fact that here the whole man is claimed for the allegiance of God. The acceptance of God's covenant is no formal requirement. It is the practical following of God's way and doing so with an inner response of affection and gladness which are part of the real acceptance of that way.

This paragraph confronts us in the modern world with a question which we ought not to avoid. Is love to God the first and great commandment? Is it urgent for every human being to love God? We cannot answer otherwise than yes, on the basis of Old Covenant or New: we must admit that love of God is not an immediate test of the worth of human life, but we must hold on to the conviction that it is the ultimate test by which human life is lifted out of its fragility and unworthiness and made great.

In v. 7 the Israelites are commanded to teach the words to their children, and to talk of them at home and abroad, and at night and morning. Faith in the one true God is the most precious inheritance and it, above all, must be communicated to the on-coming generation. The way to do this is to speak of it in the home, and to remember God at the close and at the opening of the day. Where parents care about their faith they can generally communicate its truth and importance to their children in any age.

It is not clear whether the command that the laws should be bound as signs upon the head, before the eyes, and upon the posts and gates of the house, is meant to be taken metaphorically or literally. In principle, it reinforces the importance of the fundamental faith. v. 8 became the basis for the 'Phylacteries' of the New Testament (Matt. 23.5) (Hebrew *Tephillin*). On small parchment rolls 6.4-9, 11.15-21 and Ex. 13.1-10, 11-16, were written, placed in small containers and worn on the arm and the forehead at morning prayer. So, too, a similar container called *mezuzah* was fixed at the right-hand door-post in Jewish houses and touched as people entered or left.

The temptation to forget God because of prosperity is a recurrent feature of human life. The transmission of faith and experience to a generation which has not entered into the power of the one or the discipline of the other is not always successful. What has come into being through a living faith is treated as inevitably there in human life. Each new generation needs to be recalled to its own allegiance to God. The truth is that even in diluted form, belief in God is powerful for human well-being, but in diluted form it cannot transmit itself.

It is quite clear that the message of Deuteronomy was one of the shaping influences of our Lord's own ministry. The Scriptural basis of the rebuttal of the temptations which came to him (Matt. 4.1-11; Luke 4.1-13) is to be found in 8.3 and two quotations from this present chapter vv. 13 and 16. v .13. ' Thou shalt fear the Lord thy God and shalt swear by his name ' is adapted to the situation and becomes ' Thou shalt worship the Lord thy God and Him only shalt thou serve '. God alone is the object of man's loyalty and obedience. Satan has no right to it.

The *word* FEAR used in this verse stands for the fundamental acceptance of God as God, that reverence for Deity which is essential to our acknowledgement of him. It is not to be contrasted with love, which is our response to the Deity which we recognize. In the same verse Israel is commanded to swear by the name of God. This is formally contradicted by the teaching of Jesus in Matt. 5.33-37, but it should be remembered that this is a higher standard of simple ' yes ' or 'no ' for a people which has learnt to take God as the ultimate test of truth.

The second verse in this chapter referred to by Jesus is v. 16. ' Thou shalt not tempt (that is, put to the test) the Lord your God.' The temptation is to jump from a pinnacle of the Temple and expect God to save him. The answer is that it is wrong to try to force God's hand in this way. Whatever comes in the way of obedience must be attempted, but Jesus cannot run unnecessary risks and then claim God's protection. The reference to the temptation in Massah (to which Deuteronomy refers again 9.22, 33.8) belongs to that background of tradition which this book takes for granted. The account is given in Ex. 17.1-7 of the incident in which the people demanded that Moses should give them water, and at God's command Moses struck the rock at Horeb. Adam Welch thinks that vv. 16-19 are an intrusion because[4] 'the fretfulness, by which Israel provoked its God to anger at Massah, was due to sheer need, not to success or abundance. What drove the people there to complain, so far from being ready-dug wells, was their want of water.' It should, however, be remembered, that even in prosperity there may be shadows, and occasions for putting God to the test. What matters is to do what is right in the sight of the Lord and it will be well with us.

The chapter ends with a characteristic reference of the meaning of the laws which are here expounded to the redemption which God has wrought for us. A man's son will want

---

[4] *Deuteronomy: the Framework to the Code*, p. 82.

to ask the meaning of that faith which meant so much to his father. The answer is to refer to that slavery in Egypt, which itself is hateful, but which is the occasion of that redemptive action in the power of which Israel lives. The laws have their justification in the action of God for the good of Israel. ' For our good always.' That is Israel's conviction about the action of God. The word of St. Paul (Rom. 8.28 R.S.V.) ' We know that in everything God works for good with those who love him, who are called according to his purpose', is deeply based on Old Testament conviction. This word is repeated in the phrase AND IT SHALL BE RIGHTEOUSNESS UNTO US—the preservation and furtherance and blessing of life.

### 7.1-26  The calling and blessing of Israel

      1-5    No compromise with heathenism
      6-11   The calling of Israel
      12-16  The blessings of the faithful God
      17-24  God will cast out the nations before Israel
      25-26  Israel must be faithful at all costs

**1-5.** No compromise with heathenism. This as a policy for the dealings of one nation with another is horrifying, and doubly horrifying because it is associated with the worship of the true God. Matthew Henry comments: ' The confining of this commission to the nations here mentioned plainly indicated that after-ages were not to draw this into a precedent; this will not serve to justify those barbarous wars which gave no quarter. How agreeable so ever this method might be, when God himself prescribed it, to that dispensation under which such multitudes of beasts were killed and burned in sacrifice; now that all sacrifices of atonement are perfected in and superseded by the great propitiation made by the blood of Christ, human blood is become perhaps more precious than it was, and those that have most power, yet must not be prodigal of it.'

We cannot take refuge in this position to-day, though we may note that Matthew Henry at least did not take this passage as a model for international relations. Apart from the question of humanity, the issue which it raises for us is the relation between principle and human relationships in daily life. Loyalty to God is of course of the greatest importance, and we cannot expect never to give offence in doing this. But it is possible to offend against the corporate life of mankind by insisting unnecessarily on religious principle, and by failing to recognize that Christian and non-Christian share a common life in which both must, within limits, work together.

The urgent necessity of this is plain when we consider marriage. Marriage between people of different religious faiths has always raised problems. But a rigid ban sets up an artificial barrier which is unsatisfactory on both sides. Both fidelity to deep religious principle and common life and fellowship with all sorts and conditions of men are essential.

**6-11.** The positive side of no compromise with heathenism is the calling of Israel. This is a dangerous idea because it leads easily to the idea that, as God has chosen Israel, he is not interested in any other nation; and that to be chosen of God is to be the recipient of God's bounty, to be favoured of God more than any other.

But Israel is called to be the bearer of God's witness to himself. This is not an election to privilege, if by privilege is meant the right to be served. It is a call to hard and unremitting service from which there is no discharge. The only question here can be a question of fact. Has Israel been so called and commissioned by God? This applies equally to the Church of Christ. There is here no repudiation of the life and witness of other nations, or even the life and witness of other faiths, but simply the assertion that what is good in them must receive its justification in the light of that witness in which God has declared the meaning of his holy Name.

And here in the Old Covenant we have the assertion of that principle of justification by faith so determinative of Christian perspective. Israel has been chosen, not because of its greatness or goodness, but because of the love and faithfulness of Israel's God. To whatever extent man falls away from the image of God which he bears, the faithfulness and truth of our Covenant God remain our certain hope.

But for Deuteronomy love and hate are equal and opposite. God hates as much as he loves. We have been taught in the New Covenant that the hostility of God towards sin is always an instrument in the service of his love. There runs through the teaching of Jesus a note of dread for those who go counter to the will of God, but also a note of gratitude for the generosity of God towards the unthankful and evil: and we must bear this in mind as we read Deuteronomy.

**12-16** expound one of the favourite themes of the Deuteronomist—the blessings of the faithful God. They are seen here as fertility and absence of disease. These are natural blessings which mankind looks for. In barren lands, or near to barren lands, fertility is the breath of life. In disease-ridden lands freedom from illness is the very condition of the enjoyment of existence. Here, to cope successfully with the practical tasks of life is to have the blessing of God. This is too unsophisticated a position and experience disproved it. The evil flourish as a green bay tree, while the righteous are afflicted with many troubles. Whatever determines competence at meeting the immediate requirements of life, it is not religious faith, and this must be fully and frankly acknowledged.

But there is a special blessing which the faithful God gives to his people. However much others may despise or neglect it, to his followers the characteristic blessing of God is the savour of life, and it is urgently necessary for the true mastery of life's problems.

It is unfortunate that in this section the passage turns from love to hate, and has the dreadful phrase: 'THINE EYE SHALL HAVE NO PITY UPON THEM.' Matthew Henry makes the conflict between Israel and the nations signify our inward struggle against sin, and so no question of pity arises. 'Thus we are commanded,' he says, 'not to let sin reign, nor to indulge ourselves in it, or give countenance to it, but to hate it and strive against it; and then God has promised that sin shall not have dominion over us (Rom. 6.12-14), but that we shall be more than conquerors over it.' But this is not the literal meaning, which is the antithesis of what the Gospel stands for. However deep conflict between men and women may go, we,

E

whose hope is the divine compassion, must never let our compassion fail or our pity dry up.

**17-24** contain a lesson which we must heed. We cannot assent to the picture of Israel as a war-like nation with a fierce God at her heart striking terror into all the nations on the earth. Still, the temptation of all religious groups is to be frightened at all the obstacles lying ahead of them, and to lay far too little weight upon the presence and power of God with them. 'By their fruits ye shall know them,' said our Lord. If we proclaim Christ as the hope of the world, we are bound to show what his presence in the life of the Church means. If Christ be with us, who can be against us? Unless the empowering presence of Christ enables us to overcome difficulties, to set our hands to tasks that daunt others, we have nothing to offer to the world.

**25-26.** The chapter ends with an exhortation not to covet the gold and silver of idolatrous worship. They are contaminated, and must be destroyed. The principle of this is right. We are constantly tempted to serve God and mammon. Because we do not want to be strait-laced, we tend to forget the sacrifice we ought to make. Some things, good in themselves, have such evil associations that we must stand out from sharing in them. We must not overdo this, but we must remember that faith grows by the acceptance of indispensable sacrifices.

### 8.1-20   The meaning of life is dependence on God

     1-5    The discipline of the desert
     6-10   The promised land
     11-18  The temptation to forget God
     19-20  The penalty of forgetting God

**1-5.** There are many accounts of the wanderings of Israel in the desert, and they emphasize different aspects of the experience. Was it a time when Israel at its worst defied God so that not until every one of the rebellious generation—with only two exceptions—had died out could Israel take up again the march to the Promised Land? Ps. 106 makes the story one of unremitting rebellion. Or was it a time when Israel was so intimate in its fellowship with God that it really understood God, and did his will then and at no other time? This is the picture presented to us by Hosea and Jeremiah.

The stories cannot be equally true in all respects, but they may both be true in some respect. The story of difficulty and rebellion may refer partly to the actual experience and also to the absolute standards of a later age, and the story of intimate fellowship, truth realized in reflection upon the experience. We can be grateful that in this book, which is apt to think in terms of black and white, there is this picture of God using the discipline of life to bring his people to acknowledge his way.

And what has Israel learnt from this experience in the wilderness? To accept life at the hands of God. To know that, whether it was manna that sustained them, or other food to which they were more accustomed, it all proceeded from the hands of the one creative and reigning God.

This is the third passage from Deuteronomy quoted in the account of the temptation of Jesus. Luke 4.4 simply quotes 'Man shall not live by bread alone'; Matt. 4.4 adds 'but by every word that proceedeth out of the mouth of God'. This gives a slightly different meaning to the Hebrew, following the Septuagint translation 'every word' for the Hebrew 'every thing'. In this account the distinction is not between the different ways in which God feeds his people, but between the material food and the spiritual guidance of God. But on either interpretation, the meaning is that God is the true sovereign of all life, and only by following him shall we live rightly. The ministry of Jesus derives its strength not from independent action, but from humble dependence upon God.

**6-10.** The experience of the desert was a testing one—not pleasant at the time. It was a preparation for the enjoyable experience of sharing in the Promised Land—a good land, a land of brooks of water, of fountains and depths, springing forth in valleys and hills. The fertility of Palestine was much greater in earlier times than now, and it was certainly a good land as it presented itself to the escaped slaves from Egypt, or later to the Israelites in captivity in Babylon. The contrast between discipline and enjoyment is essential to the passage.

(v. 10 both expresses and justifies the basis of the Jewish and Christian practice of thanksgiving for food.)

'The Promised Land' is one of the permanent images of faith, and the extension of the original meaning can be taken in many forms. It is natural to think of the deliverance from the captivity of sin into the fellowship of Christ in terms borrowed from the experience of Israel. This took place in the New Testament itself. W. L. Knox comments on Rom. 6.[5] 'In Rom. 6 . . . the death and Resurrection of Jesus replace the Exodus from Egypt. The proselyte, through circumcision and the proselyte's bath, was enabled to come out of Egypt and pass through the Red Sea into the promised land of Israel. . . . Paul transfers the argument to the death and Resurrection of Jesus. Those who share in it through faith and pass through the waters of Baptism are delivered from the old Egyptian bondage to sin and pass instead into a new slavery to righteousness which results in sanctification.'

But as is abundantly clear from vv. 11-18 of this chapter, any conception of the Promised Land, short of the ultimate Kingdom of God, is beset by the danger and reality of people falling away from their true allegiance. Matthew Henry says hopefully: 'Whatever others saw, it is probable that Moses saw in it a type of the better country: the Gospel Church is the New Testament Canaan, watered with the Spirit in his gifts and graces, planted with the trees of righteousness. Heaven is the good land, in which there is nothing wanting, and where there is a fulness of joy.' This of course belongs not to Moses, but to inevitable Christian imagery. So we read of the heroes of faith (Heb. 11.16, 13.14) that 'they desire a better country, that is, a heavenly: wherefore God is not ashamed to be called their God: for he hath prepared for them a city.' The Promised Land beckons us on. It is no will-o'-the-wisp; for it rests on the faithfulness of God.

**11-18.** Prosperity is likely to undo all that has been learnt of God's delivering hand. Man falls into the deadliest sin of pride. 'THINE HEART BE LIFTED UP,' we read, 'AND THOU FORGET.' Israel is no longer afraid, but secure: and the

[5] *St. Paul and the Church of the Gentiles*, pp. 97-8.

memory of that time when under urgent necessity the reality and power of God to bless was the one certainty, has faded. The experience of the desert, for all its harshness, was in some ways more surely grounded in the right relation to God than the wealth and security of the Promised Land. The remembrance of the discipline has faded, until in the end we come to say ' MY POWER AND THE MIGHT OF MINE HAND HATH GOTTEN ME THIS WEALTH '. God is forgotten. We think ourselves master of our own life and destiny.

**19-20.** This is shameful; but it is not only shameful. Deuteronomy asserts that it is the way of destruction. To forget God, to stop following him, is the way of doom. God is very patient, but there is such a thing as destruction. Can we be sure that this is a word that is dead and done for? Is there not a chance that it is alive and true?

We recall the words of George Adam Smith:[6] ' The course of Divine Providence in Syria has not been one of mere development and cultivation, of building and planting. It has been full also of rebuke and frustration, of rooting up and tearing down. Judgment has all along mingled with mercy. Christ himself did not look forward to the history of the kingdom which he founded as an unchecked advance to universal dominion. He took anything but an optimist's view of the future of his Church. He pictured himself not only as her king and leader to successive victories, but as her judge: revisiting her, and finding her asleep; separating within her the wise from the foolish, the true from the false, the pure from the corrupt, and punishing her with sore and awful calamities. Ought we to look for these visitations only at the end of the world? Have we not seen them fulfilled in the centuries? Has not the new Israel been punished for her sin, as Israel of old was, by the historical powers of war, defeat, and captivity? '

Our lives are uncertain, and we are not always the best of judges of the things that belong to our peace. If once we have come to the knowledge that our life depends on God, we must pray for strength to be kept in that knowledge, and to resist

[6] *Historical Geography of the Holy Land*, pp. 112-13.

the delusions of immediate success. In God is our strength and hope.

### 9.1-7   Israel's success is due, not to itself, but to God
            1-3    The action of God
            4-5    The wickedness of the dispossessed
            6-7    Israel a stiff-necked people

Moses here speaks to Israel about to cross the Jordan and face peoples, whom they think of as giants, but who will not be able to stand before them. This is because Yahweh their God has gone before them as a devouring fire.. The Deuteronomist has no qualms about the destructive action of God: he builds on the fact of dispossession which is long past. The action of God in going before his people is fundamental to belief in the living God. However strange and terrible the situations to which we may come, God has come there before us.

Israel is not to think of this conquest as due to its own righteousness, but as due to God's promise and the wickedness of the nations who are dispossessed. This is too simple a theory of history to account for the facts. Faith in the true God and moral obedience is not enough to account for historical success. Faith in God and moral living will, other things being equal, be a powerful factor in national stability and achievement. The absence of a unifying faith and the growth of moral corruption will be a source of instability and failure. Yet the energy of faith and conduct relevant to historical achievement will not always be faith in God, and faith in God may lack elements necessary for historical achievement. Yet the conviction of the Deuteronomist that there is a wickedness which spells defeat, and a righteousness which means success, though not vindicated literally in the process of history is a conviction which we cannot altogether let go, and must expect to be vindicated in the ultimate Kingdom of God.

The conquest was not due to Israel's righteousness. Israel is in fact a stiff-necked people. The metaphor is that of an animal that will not go in the way his master wants to drive him. And the Deuteronomist takes us back to Horeb to show us Israel's stubborn rebellion. 'Ye have been rebellious against the Lord from the day that I knew you,' we are going to be told.

Are we right to think of Israel as A STIFF-NECKED PEOPLE? Or is this a product of an over-exacting conscience? Israel was, after all, the bearer of the witness to Yahweh its God; by its faithfulness that witness has been transmitted down to the present day. Is it not rather neurotic to dwell on Israel's faults? And is not this perpetuated in the New Testament when we read in the speech of Stephen (Acts 8.51): 'Ye stiff-necked and uncircumcised-in heart and ears, ye do always resist the Holy Ghost: as your fathers did, so do ye?'

This is an important question. On the answer to it depends much of our estimate of Biblical truth. That the over-emphasis on this aspect of Biblical truth can be neurotic we ought not to deny. But to repudiate it in principle, is to repudiate the reality of God. There is a difference between what we say to other human beings, and what we say to God. In the presence of perfection, we are constantly being put in the wrong. It is understandable that people should think that the presence of perfection involves a strain that humanity cannot bear, yet the awareness of the gulf between an achievement and God's demand has in Biblical faith acted not to belittle human possibilities, but to enhance them.

## 9.8-10.11 Narrative Illustration: The stubborn heart of Israel shown at Horeb in the episode of the Molten Bull

| | |
|---|---|
| 8-11 | God gives Moses two tables of stone |
| 12-14 | God purposes to destroy Israel because of its sin |
| 15-17 | Moses sees the molten bull, and breaks the stone tables |
| 18-20, 25-29 | Moses intercedes for Israel and Aaron |
| 21 | Moses destroys the molten bull |
| 22-24 | Other occasions of Israel's sin |
| 10.1-5 | God gives two new tables of stone and Moses puts them back into the ark |

6-7    Part of the journey of Israel
8-9    The ministry of Levi
10-11  God accepts the prayer of Moses

We turn back from Moab to Horeb to hear the Deuteronomic account of the episode of the molten bull which repeats many of the words of the mainly earlier account given
in Ex. 32-34. (We are familiar with the image as the golden
calf: but the gold spoken of in Exodus is not mentioned in
Deuteronomy: and the Hebrew word translated 'calf' means
'a young bull just come to maturity'.) In the picture of Horeb
which Deuteronomy gives us, we have not only the Revelation
of God, and the people's love and obedience (as in chapter 5),
we have also the people's sin.

The account in Exodus is more vivid and interesting; the
account here is more formal, in keeping with the Deuteronomic
style. Here, also, the account is rather confused, and may
well be the product of different hands, with interpolations.

Though the episode of the molten bull is securely grounded
in the complete tradition, it is difficult to think that it is
historical. It presupposes that we take the second commandment against the making of images as in force at the time of
Moses; and that we ignore the similarities between this story
—especially as given in the account in Exodus—and the
account of the bull images set up by Jereboam (I Kings
12.26-33).

The story is a story of the 'wrath' of God. How is it
possible for God to bear with the sin of man? Why does he
not destroy man altogether? Why does he not blot out their
name from under heaven? It is this concern which finds
expression in the story of the flood (Gen. 6-9).

Here the wrath of God is abated by the intercession of
Moses (cp. 3.23-29). The greatest word in the intercession of
Moses given in Exodus, and probably a later addition there
(Ex. 32.31-32) is not given here. Moses says: 'Oh, this peonle
have sinned a great sin, and have made them gods of gold.
Yet now, if thou wilt forgive their sin—; and if not, blot me,
I pray thee, out of thy book which thou hast written.' While
we must not read into this the context of eternity given in the

New Testament, we must admit that here is selfless concern at its finest for the well-being of the people he leads.

The prayer given here (9.26-29) follows and adapts Ex. 32.11-13. The underlying concern is for the glory of God. If Yahweh has to destroy Israel, will it not reflect upon his greatness? Is he the true God and able to deliver his people? In the last resort this and the appeal to compassion for the wretchedness of Israel are identical with one another. We ought not to oppose God's glory and his love, as if they had nothing to do with each other. The love of God is rooted in what he is. To appeal to the glory of God is not to appeal to impersonal majesty, but to the immensity of his eternal being in which his love is grounded. It is because of what God is, not because of what we are, that intercessions have prevailing power with him.

We must take the wrath of God against the sin of man seriously. In a well-known hymn, the writer, having begun a verse rightly

> There is no place where earth's sorrows
> Are more felt than up in heaven;

continues his thought on an emptier plane:

> There is no place where earth's failings
> Have such kindly judgment given.

The judgment of God is compassionate, but it is also costly. It is not kindly, as though he minimized the sin or his own wrath, but redemptive, and he himself bears the cost of the hatefulness of sin. In so far as this incident is analogous to the fact of the Cross, it is to be noted that the identification of God with the intercessor is complete in the Christian story. It is God whose love moves him to lift his people out of his anger. This is true—though not so clearly true—of the Old Testament also, because the prophetic and priestly word which is given passionate utterance in Moses is certainly given by God.

The reason why Moses broke the two tables of stone (9.17) is a little obscure. Moses seems to have shared in the anger of

God at the sin of the people. A people who show such in-gratitude to their God do not deserve the privilege of having these laws, and Moses destroys their possession of them. It has been suggested that the story originated to teach that the loss of the second two tables of the law did not matter greatly, because they were only a copy of the divine original. But in the accounts the new copy of the laws is as divine as the original.

The repetition of the forty days and forty nights (9.9, 18, 25, 10.10)—the traditional period of meditation—is a sign of the composite character of the narrative. The sentence in 9.19, THE LORD HEARKENED UNTO ME THAT TIME ALSO, is probably an editorial addition. It is difficult to give it any clear meaning.

The reference to Aaron in v. 20 is much shorter than in the account in Exodus, but it is also much sharper. There is no special prayer for Aaron in Exodus, but also, he is not made to bear the special anger of God.

In vv. 22-23 we have four instances of Israel's rebellion against God. MASSAH—the putting of God to the test of which an account is given in Exodus 17.1-7—was mentioned in 6.16, and an account of the sin at Kadesh-barnea was given in 1.19-35. The other two incidents are recorded in Num. 11. One is Taberah, the place of burning, where the fire of the Lord is said to have burnt up part of the camp, when the people were complaining; the other is Kibroth-hattaavah (the graves of craving) where the people had a craving for the food they used to eat in Egypt, and a plague fell on them when they were eating a plentiful supply of quails.

1-5 give an account of the making by Moses of the Ark. The Ark was one of the most ancient religious symbols of Israel. It embodied the presence of Yahweh among his people. The force of this is seen from Num. 10.35-36, ' And it came to pass, when the Ark set forward, that Moses said, Rise up, Lord, and let thine enemies be scattered; and let them that hate thee flee before thee. And when it rested, he said, Return, O Lord, unto the many thousands of Israel.'

This account in Deuteronomy probably rests on an earlier

version which has been set aside by the later version given in Exodus. There the Ark was an elaborate construction made by Bezaleel (37.1-9) see 25.10-21, 31.1-11, 35.30-36.1. Here the construction is very simple. The Ark was made of acacia, that is, hard wood. The purpose of this account may be to lessen the importance of the Ark by making it a simple container of the tables of the law. It is not certain whether THERE THEY BE refers to the time of Moses or the Deuteronomist. We do know the Ark was believed to contain the tables of the law till at least the time of Solomon (cp. I Kings 8.9).

**6-7** are an intrusion into the narrative, and contain an obscure part of Israel's itinerary. In Num. 33.31-33 we have names sufficiently similar to be considered the same, but we are not much wiser. According to the later account in Num. 20.22-29 followed in 32.50 Mount Hor was the place of Aaron's death.

**8-9** give the setting apart of the tribe of Levi to perform priestly functions. Three are mentioned here: (1) TO BEAR THE ARK OF THE COVENANT OF THE LORD (cp. 3.19); (2) TO STAND BEFORE THE LORD AND MINISTER (cp. 18.1-8); and (3) TO BLESS (cp. 21.5). There is evidence that originally the tribe of Levi had no priestly functions (cp. Gen. 49.5-7): perhaps the earlier tradition of Horeb which Deuteronomy followed set apart the tribe of Levi for priestly functions. The late tradition, foreshadowed in Ezek. 40-48 and embodied in Ex. 28-29 and Num. 3-4, made a sharp distinction between priests and Levites. Here all Levites are priests and their inheritance is not land, but their share in the religious offerings. The Deuteronomic law is given in 18.1-8.

The passage concludes with the assent of God to Moses' intercession, and a command to journey into the Promised Land.

**10.12-22 The requirement of God**

12-15 to fear and love him

16-19 to imitate him

20-22 to be grateful to him

We come back from the reminder that Israel has a stubborn

heart—exemplified by its disobedience at Horeb itself—to the acknowledgement that in God is all our hope. This passage may be compared with Micah 6.1-8, which it recalls. Both passages insist that what God requires is in principle something simple, which the humblest can do.

Three requirements are asked for here.

1st (12-15) we must fear and love God. This combination of fear and love is the strength of Biblical faith. By fear is not meant abject terror, but reverence for God as God. God is not only personal, he is also other than man. In all God's love of us and our love of him, there is the fact that he is God and we are men.

Christians are sometimes too much influenced by I John 4.18: ' There is no fear in love; but perfect love casteth out fear because fear hath torment. He that feareth is not made perfect in love.' There is a fear which is a blemish upon true love, because it shows itself in half-hearted trust. God is such that we can trust him utterly. But there is a fear, as the Bible uses the word, which is not a blemish on our love, but its indispensable complement.

God is not another person or thing on the same plane as those about us. He has an absolutely unique relation to us. We need a word to indicate the full recognition of his presence. It is the strength of the Deuteronomic testimony to combine insistence on the need to recognize God as God with an equal insistence that our response to him is one of intimate acknowledgement and affection.

This corresponds to something in God himself. THE HEAVEN AND THE HEAVEN OF HEAVENS IS THE LORD'S THY GOD. All the immensity of creation belongs to God, and he is beyond and above it all. But God has entered into a special relationship of affection with this people to whom we belong. Within God's people we can know the full meaning of his electing love. He is not only God. He is our God, and we are his people.

2nd (16-19) we must imitate God. Our imitation must begin in a humility which imitates the humility of God, who, though he is so great, is concerned to succour the weak and helpless.

We are familiar with the thought of the Incarnation as the expression of a humble-minded God stooping down to share the lot of man and to take his life upon him. But the humility of God is central to the Old Covenant too.

Man's trouble is that through his pride he will not share in all the greatness that the way of God would open out to him. We have here two metaphors of humility, one the circumcision of the heart (cp. 30.6 and Jer. 4.4) and the other ceasing to be stiff-necked. Both imply the taking away of false pride that would prevent our entering whole-heartedly into the purposes of God.

God is indeed utterly supreme. He is GOD OF GODS AND LORD OF LORDS (a phrase later adopted for the Christ of the Book of Revelation 19.6). He is so great that he has no need to be impressed by the power and prestige of human beings or by the hope of gain, as men are constantly tempted to be. He is above and beyond the unrighteousness and uncharitableness of men. This is fundamental to the meaning of the Old Covenant. So when Peter wakes up to the fact that in Christ the division between Jew and Gentile has broken down, he puts it in terms of a new understanding of the faith in which he had been nurtured. 'Of a truth,' he said, 'I perceive that God is no respecter of persons' (Acts 10.34).

And the characteristic action of God in delivering Israel from Egypt when they were utterly helpless must be imitated in doing acts that are just, even to the point of being generous towards the fatherless, the widow and the stranger (see note on 1.16). God is on their side and pleads their cause. Righteousness before him is that succouring righteousness which champions the cause of the oppressed. Israel knows the experience of being a stranger in a strange land. It knows, too, the compassion of God in that experience. It is for Israel to act as the channel of God's compassion towards the stranger in their midst.

3rd (20-22) we must be thankful to God. The redeeming acts of God are not only a guide to conduct, they are the source of our joy and pride in life. All our life is lived in gratitude for what God has done for us.

God, the Deuteronomist insists, is our ultimate loyalty. We must fear and serve him. But this again in no distant manner, but in an intimate bond that goes to the very roots of our being. On him we depend utterly. HE IS THY PRAISE, we are told; if there is any worth in us, it is because of him. If we should fail, or be unworthy, he can renew us. But if he should fail, the meaning of our life is taken away. In praising him, we are acknowledging the wonder of him whose grace is the source of our well-being. God has done for us the great and terrible things on which our lives depend.

What the Deuteronomist has in mind is the grimmer side of the Exodus. But as we give it a wider application, we cannot deny that the scale of the Christian Gospel is greater than we ourselves can measure. The immensity of God's love and power as he has declared it in the Bible is in some ways more frightening in its depth and range than we often admit. Yet the purpose of all God's acts is to bring us into fellowship with himself. Israel which reverences the mighty God does so with immeasurable gratitude for his enabling love—seventy persons went down into Egypt, and now they are as the stars of heaven in number.

Adam Welch says of this conviction that the God of illimitable power has elected Israel out of his free grace:[7] 'It is this conviction which gives the motive for the "fear and great joy" (Matt. 28.8) which are expected to characterize the people's temper of mind, as they characterized the disciples after the Resurrection. Fear and joy are not the two poles round which Israel's mind is to move: fear and joy are blended together, because the great deeds which prove Yahweh's power are the deeds which he has wrought on their behalf (10.21). The conviction of the Almighty as Israel's God is the basis of all the Deuteronomic ethics.'

## 11.1-32　Obedience or disobedience to God the fundamental choice

### 1-9　Those who have seen the disciplinary acts of God must obey him

[7] *The Religion of Israel under the Kingdom*, p. 216.

The last chapter of exhortation before the giving of the laws dwells on the sterner side of God's dealings with men. Israel is exhorted to obedience, but obedience which is fully conscious of the unhappy results of disobedience. The Hebrew word *musar* in v. 2 means 'discipline', which may in fact be deep enough to amount to 'chastisement', but which is designed to bring back Israel to trust in and obedience to the love of God.

The author of this section makes a distinction between the generation which has seen, and their children who have not known. The actual experience of God's discipline must be transmitted to govern Israel's history. Two experiences in particular are mentioned—one external, the destruction of Pharaoh and his army; the other internal, the destruction of rebels against the way God is leading his people.

Pharaoh, king of Egypt, little knew what he was doing when he set his will against the will of the eternal God—and there came upon him a fearful ruin. Dathan and Abiram led a secular revolt against the way in which God was leading his people through Moses, and they were swallowed up in the midst of all Israel. The account of this latter incident is given in Num. 16. In this chapter earlier and later accounts are woven together, the earlier one mentioned Dathan and Abiram alone, the later one dealt with the revolt of Korah—a revolt of Levites claiming equality with the priesthood. This latter story was not known to the Deuteronomist because it pre-supposes a later historical situation. These stories in their combined form were accepted later as the classical examples of unlawful rebellion (cp. Augustine, *City of God* 9.8: 'The seditious, separating themselves from the society ordained by God, were by the earth swallowed up quick, to invisible pains for a visible example.')

These examples are meant to teach Israel that the way of
disobedience to God means disaster. The truth of this is
independent of the fact that the historical facts underlying
the incidents are capable of more than one explanation. Disobedience to the established institutional organization is too
easily identified with disobedience to God. But this does not
mean that disobedience to God can be treated lightly. It is
essential to any living hold of faith in God that God should
not be mocked by those who rebel against him. We may see at
the moment the wicked triumphing in and because of his
wickedness, and have to bear it. What we cannot bear, if we have
faith in God, is that nothing is ever done about it, and that at
the end of the day wickedness still triumphs and gets away with
it. The word of Deuteronomy still stands, that the way of
disobedience to God is the way of disaster.

In vv. 10-17 we are told that God has a specially close
relation to Israel's land. By contrast with the land of Egypt,
where the fertility obviously depends upon the human irrigation
schemes, the fertility of Palestine depends upon incalculable
rainfall. If Israel loves God and keeps his commandments,
then God will send the rain the land needs. But if Israel is
disobedient, God will shut up the heaven against them and the
land will perish from drought. The mention (v. 10) of watering
seeds with the foot, probably refers to the working of a water-
wheel. In Palestine, the whole of the winter is the rainy
season; but the rains start in October, and the late rains in
March and April are specially necessary for the harvest.
George Adam Smith[8] says: 'The climate of Egypt does not
suggest a personal Providence, but the climate of Palestine
does so.'

Has this passage any word to say to-day? We cannot think
that God sends or withholds rain in accordance with people's
obedience to him. Indeed, we have the highest authority for
denying it. 'He maketh his sun to rise on the evil and the good,
and sendeth rain on the just and the unjust' (Matt. 5.45). Can
we then equate the controllable with the human, and the un-

---

[8] *Historical Geography of the Holy Land*, p. 73.

controllable with the divine? Not in any crude form, but in principle yes. Man's achievement is in principle precarious, and depends for its stability in binding into human activity that transcendent factor which he cannot control, but which controls him. Some factors in the precariousness of human achievement have rightly been eliminated by science. Faith in God does not depend upon opposing the strengthening of human stability where it can be strengthened, but upon the recognition that, however strengthened, it remains inherently precarious and needing that succour which God alone can give it. The withholding of the blessing of God is man's destruction.

**18-20** repeat 6.6-9 with very little change. The way of obedience to the living God is fundamental to life, and his paths of righteousness must be transmitted to the oncoming generation, and must be a normal and pervasive feature of adult life. This is the basis of Israel's security (we remember that vv. 13-21 with 6.4-9 and Num. 15.17-31 form the Jewish *Shema*ᶜ appointed to be read night and morning).

The blessing of God is given in terms that are now familiar (cp. 2.25, 7.24). Israel will dispossess mightier nations than itself, and the ideal limits of the lands from the wilderness in the south to Lebanon in the north, and from the river Euphrates in the east to the western sea, that is, the Mediterranean. The promise is limited by the phrase EVERY PLACE WHEREON THE SOLES OF YOUR FEET SHALL TREAD. God has had a larger purpose for Israel than Israel has historically been able to achieve. No man shall be able to stand before Israel: God will lay the dread of Israel upon the inhabitants. Israel had, in fact, a mightier inheritance—to be the servant of God in bringing all men to him: but that is hidden from the Deuteronomist.

The emphasis on the punishment of disobedience should not hide from us the fact that the theme of the book is the blessing of obedience. God wants to bless the people whom he has chosen. We read in the New Testament: 'God sent not his son into the world to condemn the world, but that the world, through him, might be saved.' The same principle holds here

F

also. It is blessing that God wants to bring upon his people, and here is their opportunity of receiving it.

The central point of the chapter, indeed of this whole section of preaching, comes in vv. 26-28. To obey the commandments of God means blessing; to go after other gods, and disobey the way of the true God means curse (cp. chaps. 27-30). There is a moral demand at the heart of life, and it must be faced and accepted by each new generation. The terms in which Deuteronomy thinks of the blessing and the curse are inadequate either to the complexity of life or to the profundity of the Gospel. But their real existence is certain. This is the heart of the book; and if it is not relevant to us, we may jettison it. But it presents itself anew in each age. To go with God is the way of life: to go against God is the way of death. The Gospel of Christ clarifies the terms of that disjunction. It in no way abolishes either the demand or the promise. Man is free to reject God, but he cannot insist that this makes no difference. If he rejects God, he builds a life determined by that rejection, and must accept the consequences of going against the structure of his own being and the nature of the universe.

In vv. 29-30 we have the command to put the blessing on Mount Gerizim—the south or right-hand side of the land—and the curse on Mount Ebal—the north or left-hand side. The two hills face one another with a deep valley in between, in which is Shechem 'the natural capital of these highlands'. 'Nothing comes with greater surprise upon the visitor to Palestine,' says George Adam Smith,[9] 'than to discover that with her advantage of defence, Jerusalem lies on a barren, awkward site, and that natural and historical precedence have to be given, not to Mount Sion and the City of David, but to Mounts Ebal and Gerizim, with Shechem between.'

What does to PUT THE BLESSING AND THE CURSE ON THESE MOUNTAINS mean? It means to have the blessing and curse proclaimed there, and thus to have the mountains associated in imaginative feeling with what has been solemnly affirmed upon them. There, it would seem, in the very structure of the

[9] *Historical Geography of the Holy Land*, p. 331. cp. 117-21.

land is the call from God to choose between where their
allegiance belongs. This passage is obviously later than the
time of Moses, and presupposes the events described in
chapter 27, where the people undertook the obligations of the
laws and set up the monument to it. That witness is still
there, and the speaker makes reference to it. The geographical
references in v. 30 are very confused. The passage ends with
a reference to the passing of Israel over Jordan to possess the
land, and the need to keep all the laws now being proclaimed.

## *PART TWO*

### THE DEMANDS OF THE COVENANT
### 12.1-26.19

### III

### RELIGIOUS INSTITUTIONS
### 12.1-17.7

**12.1-28  The one centre of true worship**
      1 The general title of the laws
      2-7 The law of the central sanctuary
      8-12 The removal of the wrong habits
      13-19 Repetition of the demand and implications of
          the law
      20-28 The relaxation in social customs involved

Of the laws embodied in Deuteronomy, it is the law concerning
the one centre of true sacrifice which has attracted most
attention (and even if with Dr. Welch we do not attribute this
to the book as a whole it is here in this chapter). The people
of Israel are ordered to destroy all the places which had ever
been used by the Canaanites to worship their gods—to tear
down their altars, to dash in pieces their pillars (i.e. sacred
stones) and burn their groves (i.e. wooden poles; Hebrew
*Ashērim,* see 16.21-22). Instead of these Yahweh the God of
Israel shall appoint one place for sacrifice, and there Israel
shall bring their burnt offerings (burnt wholly upon the altar),
their sacrifices (of which the fat was burnt and the rest eaten),
their tithes, the heave offerings (lifted on by the worshippers)
and shall have a family sacramental meal.

Now the literature of the Old Testament is full of references
to the use of high places for the worship of God. An earlier

law (Ex. 20.24-26) allows many places for the worship of the God of Israel and this is taken for granted in many passages (cp. Gen. 12.6, Judg. 6, I Sam. 7, I Kings 18.19, 32, and elsewhere). By the eighth century Israel appears to have gradually appropriated shrines belonging to the country, and the prophets complain of their unfaithfulness and speak against such practices (cp. Hos. 4.12-13; Isa. 1, 29; Jer. 3, and elsewhere). But they appeal to no law, and it is clear that this new law came from the witness of the eighth-century prophets.

Sacrifices in the Old Testament were offered for three main purposes; as gifts to the Deity, as a means of union with him, and as a means of everlasting life.[1]

The characteristic of the sacrifices mentioned in Deuteronomy is that they are eucharistic—thanksgiving for the gifts of God to his people. As Buchanan Gray says:[2] 'The gifts of Yahweh to Israel ought to call up feelings of gratitude and joy; and so in Deuteronomy sacrifice is pre-eminently regarded as a joyful feast eaten before Yahweh and in remembrance of what he has done. To sacrifice, to eat before Yahweh, to rejoice before Yahweh, have here become synonymous.' There is no trace of the later emphasis on sin and guilt offering (cp. Lev. 4.5).

In vv. 8-12 the contrast is not between the one place of true sacrifice and idolatrous worship, but between what Israel did in the wilderness and what it should do in the Promised Land. What did Israel do in the wilderness by way of sacrifices? v. 8 is sufficient to suggest that elaborate ritual in Leviticus did not exist in the time of Moses. Amos asks (v. 25) 'Have ye offered unto me sacrifices and offerings in the wilderness forty years, O house of Israel?' and expects the answer 'no'. Jeremiah mentions a word of God (7.22) which says: 'I spake not unto your fathers nor commanded them in the day that I brought them out of the land of Egypt concerning burnt offerings and sacrifices.' (But see apart from Deuteronomy Ex. 20.24: 21.29-30; 23.18-19.) Prophetic criticism of the use of sacrifice has been taken to mean that sacrifice never had any

[1] W. O. E. Oesterley: *Sacrifices in Ancient Israel*, p. 11.
[2] *Sacrifice in the Old Testament*, p. 47.

legitimate place in the religion of Israel. But if we remember
that Deuteronomy is the fruit of the teaching of the eighth-
century prophets, we shall not draw any such conclusion. The
message of Deuteronomy, certainly, is clear: the institution of
sacrifice must serve the worship of Yahweh, the God of Israel.
This is the only basis of its continuance in Israel.

The celebration here asked for is a family celebration. The
religion of the Old Testament, and of the New Testament as
rooted in it, is family worship. It is a question of ourselves
and our households rejoicing before the Lord. And the family
includes everyone. We must note the inclusion in the family
celebration of worship of the Levite. The Levite was the
original priest of the high place, dispossessed by this law of
centralization. Deuteronomy insists that the victims of economic change shall receive consideration and compensation in
the new order.

With the change in habits of worship comes a change in
relation between the secular and the sacred. There is an ancient
superstition that tribes and their gods are physically akin to
their animals, and this, among other things, encouraged the
worship of animals. So the domestic animals could not be
killed except for religious purposes, while the gazelle or the
deer (A.V. the roebuck and the hart), having no kinship with
the tribe, could be killed freely. According to this law, the
ritual regulations did not apply to ordinary food. This is in
conflict with the regulations given in 14.3-20 which are almost
identical with Lev. 11.2-23. Whether these belong to Deuteronomy seems doubtful.

The blood is not to be eaten—for the blood is the life. There
are a number of different theories to explain this. There was
from early times a strong temptation to drink the blood, and a
conscience against doing so (cp. I Sam. 14.32-35). Here the
blood is simply poured out upon the ground as water. Later,
it came to have atoning significance. In Lev. 17.11 we read:
'For the life of the flesh is in the blood: and I have given it to
you upon the altar to make an atonement for your souls: for
it is the blood that maketh an atonement for the soul.'

What was the effect of this centralization of worship? The

prophets had won a great victory in asserting that the natural powers in God's creation came from him and that thanks and praise were to be given to him alone. There must be no worship of natural powers for their own sake, and the worship of the living God must be such as was compatible with his justice and mercy.

The victory had been won in principle. But how was it to be fulfilled in practice? In the local sanctuaries scattered all over the country there were many links binding worship to the associations and practices of the gods of the original inhabitants, and to them the conservative habits of people clung. Yet the people had given allegiance to Yahweh the God of Israel, and they must be kept faithful to that allegiance. If there was one altar and one sacrifice, where the standards of worship could be carefully watched and faithfully observed, the people would be delivered from their superstitions and idolatries. The remedy was drastic, but it seemed necessary.

The centralization of sacrificial worship in part deepened its hold on the imagination of the people. But though every Israelite would hope to go to Jerusalem, the experience of sacrificial worship would not have constant impact upon the life of the people. So this legislation had the disconcerting result of creating a vacuum which came to be filled with another kind of worship, and therefore of paving the way for the supersession of sacrifice in Judaism and Christianity. The vacuum was in any case experienced in the Exile, and prayer, praise and exposition came to create the associations of worship in the local community. Centralization was in principle wrong, if it meant the attempted supersession of the local community. For the best and the worst in life the local community is the point of real action.

But what ought we to think of sacrifice? Sacrificial associations have lingered on in both Judaism and Christianity—but the practice has disappeared. In Judaism this is because of the destruction of the Temple, in A.D. 70, and the supersession of sacrifice by the requirements of the law (cp. W. D. Davies, *Paul and Rabbinic Judaism*, p. 259, where Rabbi Huna, A.D. 219-57, is quoted as saying, 'If you study the laws about sacrifice, that is to me as if you had offered them '). In Christianity this is because sacrifice has been fulfilled on an altogether different plane in the obedience of Jesus Christ to death to deliver all men from their sins.

It is hard for us across the centuries of Christian worship to enter into the frame of mind of those for whom animal sacrifice was a genuine means of entering into fellowship with the living God.

At the best, animal sacrifice was a grossly imperfect vehicle of communion with God. And this law of centralization in loosening the ties which bound the ordinary Israelite to the practice of sacrifice was used in the providence of God to bless his people. In the same way, the new relationship between secular and sacred which came about through the separation between killing for food and killing for sacrifice, led to a freer, healthier relationship of men to their world, and to a freeing of religious practice from crude superstition.

We value Old Testament sacrifice not for its own sake, but for the ideas associated with it, which were fulfilled on a higher plane in the New Testament. We cannot do justice to the faith of the New Testament, if we do not recognize how far sacrificial language has helped to shape its essential content.

But the most important question remains. What is the one centre of true worship? It is the presence of God with his people. For this many things may help, but none are indispensable. The effect of the Deuteronomic legislation, as expressed in the Josianic reformation, was almost inevitably to make the worship of Israel too national, too rigid, and too formal. It was this that formed the background of the life of Jeremiah. The result of prophetic criticism was to enlarge the understanding of the function of Israel in God's purpose, and to establish the thought of Jerusalem as the centre of true worship for the whole world (cp. Zech. 8.21; Ps. 86.9). But this is not sufficient for the purpose of God. The one centre of true worship is not a place but a person. It is in Christ (cp. John 4.19-26). For Jesus Christ seeks to gather the whole world unto himself and he is wherever his people come to him. The Deuteronomic teaching on the one centre of true worship is a limited and in part false answer to a real question. In Christ is to be found complete obedience and true freedom in worship.

## 12.29-13.18  Be faithful to the worship of the one true God

    29-32   Do not imitate the worship of other gods
    1-5     Put to death the prophet of other gods
    6-11    Put to death friends who entice to other gods
    12-18   Destroy the city that worships other gods

With this section we come more surely to the mind and heart of the Deuteronomist. Perhaps it is not all one section. It may be that 16.21-17.7 ought to come in after 12.31. And perhaps 12.32 is an intrusion. If rightly here, it is to be taken, as in Hebrew, with the three laws in chapter 13. There is indeed something odd, in a code of laws which has been added to and some of whose provisions have lapsed, about the reiteration of an injunction not to add to or diminish from it. We need the full faith in the living God maintained, not weakened, and not cluttered up with superfluous requirements. But this means free adaptation in changing situations. There is no way of ensuring this complete faithfulness by legal injunctions. Rigidity of instruction means formal rather than real obedience.

vv. 29-31 insist that the methods used in Canaanite worship are not to be used in the worship of Yahweh the God of Israel. The true God has a worship worthy of his own Name, and practices employed in relation to other gods have the taint of this alien god. One practice mentioned here is the sacrifice of children by burning. This was a common practice in the Semitic world in which the Israelites shared (cp. II Kings 16.3, 17.31, 21.6, etc.): against it the prophetic witness is emphatic (cp. 18.9-32 and the reform of Josiah, II Kings 23.10).

There is behind this injunction the vivid sense of a struggle to lift the worship of Israel free from debasing elements. Can we accept it as true universally? There is no easy way to a richer faith by the mixing of religious practices; where an alien religious practice is morally offensive to the nature of worship it is most to be repudiated; and if religious practices are borrowed they must take on the colour of their new environment.[3]

In the three laws in chapter 13 it is made clear that nothing can justify the abandonment of faith in the living God. Even if a sign or wonder given by a prophet comes to pass, this must be accepted as part of God's testing of our faith, and resisted. There is one true God and we must serve him. The false prophet must be put to death, because he has counselled rebellion against the redemptive God of Israel—and the evil must be put out of the common life.

The law about the prophet in 13.1-5 must be linked with 18.9-22, as giving the Deuteronomist's answer to the tests of true prophecy. Here the negative answer is: no prophecy can be true which undermines the faith of Israel in the living God. This is supplemented in 18.21-22 by the assertion that the word of a true prophet must be fulfilled.

The prophet is here spoken of without disrespect as a dreamer of dreams, though later, e.g. in Jer. 23.28, the prophecy given in dreams is distinguished from the morally creative word that comes from God. The question is: how can the corporate life of Israel be kept true to God? All evil must be put away. We must compare St. Paul's treatment of the man who has taken his father's wife (I Cor. 5.13).

There are two questions here of great importance. One is the testing of faith when some other attitude to life is demonstrating its power. It is easy to believe in God when it is plain that not to believe in him is to be ineffective. But when an alternative to God's way is showing great effectiveness, can we then maintain our faith? Deuteronomy says rightly that we must. However effective alternative ways of life may be, the true God has revealed himself in the redemption he has wrought for us, and we must not allow ourselves to be cheated out of our true loyalty. This is a test which is bound to arise in the life of faith. So the testing time for Christian faith is set as the time when (Mark 13.22) 'false Christs and false prophets shall arise, and shall show signs and wonders, to seduce, if it were possible, even the elect'.

The other question is: what is to be done with a false

[3] cp. *The Authority of the Faith*, Tambaram Madras Series, 1939.

prophet? The Deuteronomist's answer is quite plain—he is
to be put to death. The Deuteronomist has learnt the lesson
of the urgency of faith in the living God—he has no understanding of the meaning of tolerance. The lesson of tolerance
was only learnt by Christian minds late in Christian history
—and then only with the help of unbelievers. The fact that
the false prophet may be saying something that the defenders
of the faith may need to admit, or that in any case people do
sincerely differ on the ultimate issues of life, and that it is
barbarous to coerce in matters of faith, has not dawned upon
the Deuteronomist. He believes in a short way with unbelievers.

In vv. 6-11 the danger comes from the intimate family
circle. It may be a brother by the same mother in a house of
many wives, or a son, or daughter, or a beloved wife, or a
friend whom we would trust as we would ourselves—WHICH
IS AS THINE OWN SOUL—cp. the story of David and Jonathan,
(I Sam. 18.1, 3; 20.17)—who would persuade us to go after
other gods. The interest may be that they are near at hand
and we know them, or that they are far away and distance
adds to their enchanting power. Whoever it is they must be
resisted, and stoned to death. And what is more, though all
Israel is responsible for the stoning, our own hand must be
the first to put him to death, to show that, whatever the intimate relationship, our own loyalty to the true God is
absolutely supreme. And all Israel will hear and fear, and
stop doing these wicked things.

We have here the same principle that the only thing to do
with the signs of unbelief is to exterminate the person concerned. But there is also in a crude form the recognition that
faith in God takes precedence of all other loyalties, however
intimate, and that for the sake of that loyalty, these other
loyalties may sometimes have to be set aside. We remember
that Jesus said (Luke 14.26), 'If any man come to me, and
hate not his father, and mother, and wife, and children, and
brethren, and sisters, and his own life also, he cannot be my
disciple.'

**8. Neither shall thine eye pity him.** The enticer is neither
to be spared nor concealed. We have met this harsh treatment
before (7.16). We ought perhaps to recognize that the issue of
corporate solidarity, and latitude for the individual is both
difficult and important. When Caiaphas said (John 11.50):
'It is expedient for us, that one·man should die for the people,
and that the whole nation perish not,' he was expressing an
essential principle of national policy. When the aberrations
of individuals do not touch national security, it is easy to be
tolerant of individual fancies; but where to allow them would
threaten national well-being, it is another matter. What the
Deuteronomist has not seen is that, in spite of the urgency
of true faith, we cannot secure its presence by coercion. The
taking of some risks in allowing individual freedom is indispensable to the well-being of any community, and this is
especially true in matters of faith. But the problem of corporate solidarity in the true faith remains.

In vv. 12-18 the possibility is faced that certain worthless
people (children of Belial) have led a city to abandon its true
faith. If, after enquiry, this is found to be true, the whole
of the inhabitants of that city and all their possessions must
be destroyed. This will turn away the anger of God at their
disloyalty and renew his compassion and blessing upon
Israel.

We have met before (2.34) though in a milder .form, the
*herem* or ban, the giving of everything over to the will of the
deity by destroying it. Here we find it in its extremest form.
Nothing whatever can be left in a city which has rejected its
true faith. This, of course, is a horrifying way of attempting
to deal with religious disloyalty. The question for us is: can
we both learn to deal patiently and humanely with differences
in religious conviction and at the same time keep the note of
horror that anyone should fall away from faith in the living
God?

**18.** Note the contrast between doing what IS RIGHT IN THE
EYES OF THE LORD, and what we have found (12.8) every man
doing 'whatever is right in his own eyes'. The contrast is
not between the judgment of the community and the judgment

of the individual. It is between a person following in the way
of God, and doing what God sees to be right; and that same
person having turned away from God, and prescribing for
himself what he ought to do.

**14.1-21   Avoid customs unworthy of God's people**
  1-2    No heathen mourning customs
  3-20   Eat only clean beasts, fishes, and birds
  21     Do not eat a beast that has died, nor boil a
         kid in its mother's milk

The chapter opens with the assertion that the Israelites are
sons of God. Usually the relation between Israel and its God
is the determining factor; here every member of Israel shares
in the relation of son to father, and because of that customs
unworthy of the divine Fatherhood must be set aside. The
Old Testament does not give so much prominence to the
Fatherhood of God as the New Testament; where it does we
should notice it, and the passage catch some of the radiance
which belongs to the New Testament. 'Behold what manner
of love the Father hath bestowed upon us that we should be
called the sons of God' (I John 3.1). In v. 2 we have a
repetition of the affirmation of the election of Israel to be the
people of God (see 7.6). Israel must walk worthy of its
vocation.

There must be no cutting of the body or shaving of the eye-
brows as part of mourning rites. These practices might or
might not be justifiable in themselves, but they are associated
with an attitude to life very different from that which Yahweh
the God of Israel asks of his people. No rites can be tolerated
which imply a divided allegiance.

vv. 3-20 are almost identical with Lev. 11.2-23 (see note on
12.20-28). They have no special place in Deuteronomy, and
are certainly not mentioned in the reformation under King
Josiah (II Kings 22-23). If they form part of the original
Deuteronomy their function is to keep Israel faithful to the
one God. The original of these laws is certainly religious, not
hygienic, though A. S. Peake follows others in observing:[4]

[4] Hastings' *Dictionary of the Bible*, iv, 826.

'Where a tribe happened to regard things as unclean which
also are insanitary, it would, so far as it did so, increase its
chances with the struggle for existence, while natural selection
would tend to eliminate tribes whose ritual in no way coincided with sanitary requirements.'

Between this law and the time of the New Testament, the
laws about clean and unclean food were increased greatly,
and became a burdensome limitation on social intercourse.
In the teaching of Jesus given in Mark 7.1-23 we have a clear
repudiation of the distinction between ceremonially clean and
unclean foods. In practice neither Jesus nor his followers
made a complete and absolute breach with the law—but in
principle the revolutionary character of the teaching and action
of Jesus is plain. A. S. Peake comments: [5] ' It is clear that in
the Christian atmosphere the essentially heathen idea of ceremonial uncleaness could not survive.' And A. B. Bruce comments: [6] ' The idea throughout is that ethical defilement is alone
of importance, all other defilement, whether the subject of
Mosaic ceremonial legislation or of scribe tradition, is a trivial
affair. Jesus here is a critic of Moses as well as of the scribes
and introduces a religious revolution.'

These comments are not quite fair to the Jewish faith. The
distinction between clean and unclean, if accepted, becomes
a mark of God's people, and its practice a means of grace.
But beyond a certain limited point, such a practice is stultifying to moral insight and needs to be broken.

The injunction in v. 21 not to eat a beast that has died is
again not prescribed for reasons of hygiene, but to obey the
proper ceremonial requirements. The stranger is here regarded
as outside the community of Israel, whereas, by the later law
of Lev. 17.15 he is regarded as inside. Ex. 22.31 had said that
flesh torn by beasts should be given to the dogs. The injunction not to seethe a kid in its mother's milk, apart from offend-
ing our sense of the fitness of things, rests on a protest in the
name of the God of Israel against worshipping the natural
process of fertility. (There is a Ras Shamra text which speaks

[5] op. cit., p. 834.
[6] Expositor's Greek Testament, 1, 389.

of seething a kid in milk, though its mother's milk is not specified.)

**14.21-29 Tithes**

22-23 An annual tithe

24-27 The equivalent may be purchased at the central sanctuary

28-29 Every third year the tithe is for the Levite, the stranger, the fatherless and the widow

The payment of a tithe is a very ancient practice among non-Semitic as well as Semitic peoples. To give to God a tenth is a tangible acknowledgement of his Lordship of his creation, and of the place of religious faith in life. In this law a tithe of the product of the land, or its equivalent in money, is to be given annually, and spent in a family celebration in which the Levite shall share. (The first-born of cattle and sheep were offered at the same time.) Every three years the tithe shall be given to the Levite and with him the stranger, the fatherless and the widow.

The purpose of the tithe is said to be ' That thou mayest learn to fear the Lord thy God always '. We come to offer God worship and service because we hold his name in reverence and the very fact of doing so helps to keep alive in us that reverent devotion to him which is the spring of faith.

There is no earlier law about tithes than this. The later law found in Num. 18.21-32 : Lev. 27.30-33 reserves the tithe wholly for the Levites and makes cattle as well as agricultural produce subject to it.

In the Deuteronomic law we see how closely the worship of God and the care for the weak are bound together. It is a firm principle of that tradition in which the Christian faith has been nourished that those who believe in God shall give generously to the maintenance of his worship and service. And added to this is the conviction that true worship will show itself in the care of those who are liable to be oppressed, and in seeing that they have a real share in the opportunities of life.

In the New Testament (as, indeed, also in the best Jewish
thought) we are warned against setting the meticulous observance of every possible tithe as a substitute for the weightier
matters of the law, judgment, mercy and faith (Matt. 23.23,
cp. Luke 11.42); and also against treating the payment of
tithes and other signs of right living as a substitute for a
humble, loving, generous and obedient heart (Luke 18.9-14).

### 15.1-18  Laws of release

|       |                         |
|-------|-------------------------|
| 1-6   | Release from debt       |
| 7-11  | The ungenerous heart    |
| 12-18 | Release from slavery    |

Of these two laws of release, the first is concerned with the
remission of debt to a fellow-Israelite in every seventh year.
In v. 1 it says 'at the end of every seven years', but this is a
Hebrew idiom, and the meaning is made plain in v. 12. This
law of remission of debt is peculiar to Deuteronomy. There ·
are both earlier and later laws in Ex. 23.10-11 and Lev. 25.1-7,
according to which the land is to lie fallow in the seventh
year. In Leviticus the seventh year is called 'a sabbath of
rest unto the land' and has become known as a 'sabbatical'
year. Whether the Deuteronomic law has anything to do with
these other laws is uncertain.

This law of release applies only to the fellow Israelite.
Deuteronomy does not look to a universal community—but
within the community of Israel there is release from debt.
Opinion has been divided on whether the whole amount was
meant to be cancelled, as the words would imply, or whether
the amount was to be carried over till the following year,
which would make it more practicable. It is better to think
that the loan is intended to become a gift, especially if these
loans were simply charitable loans and not loans for business
purposes. Even so, the effect of the law, if it was ever practised, was to make people hesitate to lend money, and in the
later Jewish law, the school of Hillel enacted the Prosbul, by
which payment of all outstanding debts could be demanded.

In v. 4 we should read, 'However, there shall be no poor
among you'. This is a formal contradiction of v. 11, 'for the

poor shall never cease out of the land '. But it is a contradiction from which the man of religious faith can never escape.
In v. 4 we have the Deuteronomic faith that obedience to the
will of God will bring his blessing, and his blessing is understood as physical prosperity in which no poverty exists. This
is the faith by which the Deuteronomist lives, and by which
he asks others to live. But he is also constrained to admit that
in experience the obedience is not so complete, and the blessing is not so rich as to remove the problem of poverty
altogether. We must, in fact, be ready to act generously to
needy people. We may compare with this the contrast between the two parts of I John 2.1: ' My little children, these
things I write unto you that ye sin not: but if any man sin,
we have an advocate with the Father, Jesus Christ the righteous.' The Christian life in principle excludes sin: in practice
we have to make provision to deal with it.

The blessing of God is expressed in the words: 'thou shalt
lend unto many nations, but thou shalt not borrow; and thou
shalt reign over many nations, but they shalt not reign over
thee.' George Adam Smith comments: 'It is striking that the
fulfilment of this promise was most fully realized not while
Israel remained on their own land, but after their dispersion
among the nations, from the Greek period onwards.' He
refers to the words of Strabo quoted by Josephus:[7] 'These
Jews have penetrated to every city and it would not be easy to
find a single place in the inhabited world which has not received this race, and where it has not become master.'

But here we face an inescapable choice in interpretation.
Either this word has to be taken at its face value, and we can
look for its fulfilment in the financial dominance of the Jewish
people; or we must recognize that this is a limited and distorted view of Israel's destiny, which is to serve the world in
bringing all men to God, and that this destiny is being fulfilled
in Christ. We cannot have it both ways.

vv. 1-6 represent a concern that the poor shall be dealt with
generously in Israel. It is not clear that this particular law
was practised. But we can note that generous concern for

[7] *Antiquities*, XVI, vii, 2.

G

the well-being of the poorer members of the community which
has universal validity, and in obedience to which, as a matter
of history, Judaism has equalled if not surpassed Christianity. We read in Matt. 5.25-26 of an adversary who will not be
content until he has exacted 'the uttermost farthing'. This is
the very antithesis of the spirit of this Deuteronomic law.

Adam Welch says: [8] 'The custom of the year of release
shows the noble respect of these laws for human personality,
in the patent effort to maintain the independence of the little
man; and in the frank recognition that in order to be independent, he must possess something, some foot of ground
which gives him a standing among his fellows.'

vv. 7-11 anticipate the Sermon on the Mount, because they
penetrate behind the outward act to the intent and thought of
the heart. Obedience to God means that we have generosity
in our heart towards our brother. The Israelite is commanded
not to harden his heart against his brother. The thought is
taken up again in I John 3.17, where this hardness of heart is
reckoned a denial of the love of God. We must beware of
that selfish regard for our own interests which would make us
grudging and hostile to our brother's need.

The triangular relation between man, God, and man is made
clear by the phrase 'thine eye be evil against thy poor
brother, and thou givest him nought; and he cry unto the Lord
against thee, and it be sin unto thee'. In our relations with
our fellow-man either we come closer to God or go farther
away from him. Matthew Henry comments: 'That which we
think is our prudence, often proves sin to us.' While some
people need to curb their generosity, for the most part the
pleading of God with man is for a more generous spirit. And
what we give we must not give grudgingly but generously,
because the enjoyment of the act is what God wants and
blesses (cp. II Cor. 9.7).

vv. 12-18 gives the Deuteronomic law about slaves. A
Hebrew man or woman who has served six years must be set
free in the seventh. Not only must he be allowed to go, but
he must be equipped liberally at his master's expense. Israel

[8] *The Code of Deuteronomy*, p. 215.

was a slave in Egypt, and Yahweh redeemed him: he must
go and do likewise. If a slave of his own accord wishes to
remain, his ear—the organ of obedience—must be pierced,
and he be a slave for ever. A master must not let his slave
go grudgingly, since he has been a cheap investment—a day
labourer would have cost him twice as much.

This law does not stand by itself in the Old Testament.
An earlier law (Ex. 21.2-6) similarly sets a slave free at the
end of six years, though if he has been given a wife in slavery,
there is a strong inducement to remain a slave for the sake
of his wife and children who still belong to the master. In a
later law (Lev. 25.39-46) while an Israelite can sell himself to
another, he is not to be given the status of a slave but of a
hired servant, though he is to be released not in the seventh
year, but in the fifteenth—the Year of Jubilee. Slaves can
only be taken from other nations.

How far these laws were practised it is not easy to say.
Jer. 34.8-22 tells how, under stress of siege, the authorities in
Jerusalem proclaimed the release of slaves; and then, when
conditions had eased, withdrew the proclamation, and brought
them into captivity again. Jeremiah's indignation seems to
be directed primarily against a breach of faith rather than a
breach of the law, and vv. 13 and 14 referring to the release
of slaves in the seventh years seem a later insertion.

This law on slavery neither institutes it nor abolishes it, but
seeks to mitigate the lot of the slave. We have to recognize
that, as Ṣ. A. Cook says,[9] 'slavery in the East was not the
institution that it became in Italy or Greece or in the medieval
and modern world. The rights which a man could exercise
over his slaves did not differ so widely from those which he
held over his family.'

In general, it is not the function of religious faith to prescribe institutions, though toleration of some must come to be
recognized as inconsistent with true obedience; it is rather the
function of faith to direct the spirit in which institutions are
used. But the direction of Old Testament law is against
slavery. A slavery which lasts for only six years is not separ-

[9] *The Laws of Moses*, p. 153.

ated by an impassable barrier from freedom; and the trend
of the legislation is against slavery.

The crucial point is that the slave does not belong to a
different order from the master. He is a fellow Israelite, who,
through poverty or crime, has fallen on evil days. He is to
be treated generously and to be given a good start in freedom.
A people which remembers its own deliverance from slavery
by the mercy of God must have compassion always for those
in need.

But some do not want freedom. In the law in Exodus every
inducement is given for the slave to remain a slave; but here
the emphasis is the other way. But, even so, some would
prefer slavery. This is true to human life. Perhaps an uncertain freedom under great difficulty has less attraction than
security with good treatment. In any case, the spiritual dignity
of the ordinary man is vindicated not by the ordinary man on
his own behalf, but by men of vision, courage, and leadership
on behalf of others. And there is always resistance by a large
part of humanity to the acceptance of its own birthright.

The law ends in v. 18 with a plea for that ungrudging spirit
which no law can command. Slavery persisted because it was
profitable. But even the halving of the expenses of a hired
worker by keeping a slave for six years seemed not enough
to some masters. Deuteronomy pleads for the restraint of
evil desire by gladness in the well-being of others.

### 15.19-23  The first-born of sheep and oxen

According to this law on the first-born of sheep and oxen,
the oxen are not to be worked and the sheep are not to be
shorn. They are to be consecrated and eaten at a family meal
' in the place which Yahweh shall choose '. But if any of the
animals have a fault, they are not to be brought for sacrifice,
they are to be eaten under ordinary conditions. The earlier
law here (Ex. 13.11-16; 22.29, 30; 34.19-20) orders the offering
of the first-born on the eighth day after birth, which would be
impracticable with a central sanctuary; though the present
law too had, originally at any rate, no connection with
centralization. The later law (Num. 18.15-18) gives the whole

of the flesh to the priests, instead of allowing it to be eaten at a family feast.

The purpose of the law is to claim for Yahweh the God of Israel the processes of birth and fertility. Against the worship of fertility in itself or the ascription of it to gods with no character or history the faith of Israel set the claim of Yahweh the God of Israel to be the Lord of all things. To him, and to him alone the new-born belong. It is to be noted that on quite other grounds men are coming to a position similar to that opposed in this law—a position which gives a naturalistic explanation to the processes of birth and repudiates any transcendent moral reference. The other factor in the law is that nothing with any fault in it is to be offered to God. Nothing that men can do can be adequate to the worship of God—but man must give of his best, because only then is he truly acknowledging the claim of God as the supreme fact of life.

### 16.1-17 The Three Festivals of Israel

> 1-8     Passover with unleavened bread
> 9-12    The Feast of Weeks
> 13-15   The Feast of Booths
> 16-17   Summary

This passage gives the Deuteronomic view of the great Feasts of Israel. The word implies not only the feast but the pilgrimage to celebrate it. The earlier treatment of these feasts is given in Ex. 23.14-17; 34; 18.22-24; 12.21-27; 13.3-10, and the later treatment in Lev. 23; Num. 28-29 and Ex. 12.1-13, 14-20, 42-49; Num. 9.1-14. All strata of the laws deal with these feasts.

Their origin (with the exception of Passover, which may be nomadic) is agricultural, and belongs to the period of settlement in Palestine. In the summary the feasts are given as those of unleavened bread, weeks, and booths. (Tabernacles, the word used for booths in the A.V. means temporary resting-places.) All these feasts are connected with different stages of the harvest.

Here Passover and Unleavened Bread are combined into one feast. They were originally separate. (See Ex. 23.15 and

34.18.) Passover may have been originally an agricultural feast celebrating the appearance of the young ears of corn in the spring. In all strands of the Pentateuch it is associated with the deliverance from Egypt; in Ex. 12.27 its name (Pesah) is said to come from the meaning to pass over, because the Lord 'passed over the houses of the children of Israel in Egypt, when he smote the Egyptians'.

The law as we have it in Deuteronomy is not very clear. The passage dealing with unleavened bread breaks up the instructions about the Passover; and the mention of TENTS in v. 7 suggests that the passage partly gives a law suitable for the central sanctuary, and partly reflects an earlier time when it was celebrated near to people's homes.

In v. 6 the month of Abib is March-April—the month was called Nisan in the later Jewish Calendar. Unleavened bread could be prepared hastily for a simple meal. It is called here BREAD OF AFFLICTION because it is associated with that meal eaten in haste on the eve of the break from slavery. In v. 8 a SOLEMN assembly simply means a definitely appointed assembly. Moffatt translates it 'a day of sacred festival'.

The feast of weeks is not associated with any particular event of Israel's history: it is only linked with a general remembrance of the deliverance from Egypt. In later Jewish tradition it was associated with the giving of the law on Horeb-Sinai. It is called 'Harvest' in Ex. 23.16, and 'First fruits' in Num. 28.26. It is to be celebrated at the end of the wheat harvest. It is a family festival in which the servants, the Levite, and dependants all share. In Num. 28.27-29 the amount is prescribed—here it is a free-will offering. The offering is meant to be a gift in keeping with the prosperity of the offerer—the full amount he can afford. A free-will offering is the right basis for gifts to God—but in practice some under-estimate their own obligation and some over-estimate it.

The Feast of Booths was also called the Feast of Ingathering (Ex. 23.16-22). The 'Booths' were shelters of branches or planks often set up for those who watched vineyards. It was celebrated at the final end of the harvest, especially at the end of the vintage, probably about the end of September. In Lev.

23.43 an historical explanation is given of the feast—'that your generations may know that I made the children of Israel to dwell in booths, when I brought them out of the land of Egypt.' It again is a family celebration in which all shall rejoice.

In vv. 16-17 we have a summary of the law of the three festivals. The law is to be binding on the men—the inclusion of women and dependants to have a share in the feast is characteristic of Deuteronomy. It ends with a fine statement of the meaning of a free-will offering—EVERY MAN SHALL GIVE AS HE IS ABLE, ACCORDING TO THE BLESSING OF THE LORD THY GOD WHICH HE HATH GIVEN THEE.

The characteristic note of these festivals, for Deuteronomy, is one of rejoicing. This is specially emphasized for the last two feasts—'thou shalt be altogether joyful'. The apostle Paul speaks of rejoicing as a characteristic note of the Gospel. 'Rejoice in the Lord alway,' he writes, 'and again I say rejoice' (Phil. 4.4). But this is carrying over into the New Covenant what has already been characteristic of the Old. The worship of the living God is the source of abundant joy.

These three festivals are familiar to Christians, not only because of their place in the history of Israel, but also because they are carried forward into Christian festivals. Passover is perpetuated in the Easter Festival and in the celebration of the Communion of the Lord's Supper—the words of the Apostle being very precious: 'Christ our passover is sacrificed for us: therefore let us keep the feast, not with the old leaven, neither with the leaven of malice and wickedness; but with the unleavened bread of sincerity and truth' (I Cor. 5.1-8). The Feast of Weeks or Pentecost has been transformed into the festival of the Holy Spirit. And the feast of booths or the ingathering of the harvest has been perpetuated in Harvest Festivals, in which thanksgiving is made for the fruit of the land and the whole earth claimed for the one true God.

It is right that nature and history should be linked as in these festivals. The round of life goes on, and needs celebrating, but it does not of itself provide that wide perspective the human spirit needs. This must come from history, from great historical events acknowledged as determinative and linked with the habit of life. In modern communities our basis of life cannot be as explicitly theocratic as that of Deuteronomy, and yet the Christian festivals can be not only the festivals of the Church, but also festivals of national life, provided the events of Christian faith are acknowledged as determinative of human history. Is the life, death and resurrection of Jesus the greatest event of human history? Only if this is acknowledged to be true can Christian Festivals be a means of thanksgiving, penitence, and intercession for the whole community.

### 16.18-20    The principle of justice

These verses have intruded themselves from the section which begins in 17.8. They state the principle of justice. Because by the law of the central sanctuary the local sanctuary is no longer the seat of justice, judges and officers have to be appointed to administer it. And Deuteronomy is more concerned to lay down principles than to prescribe details.

The injunction is addressed to all Israel, who are together responsible to see that justice shall be done. Justice is to be done to those who cannot forcibly secure it for themselves (cp. 24.17 and 27, 19, where the wresting of judgment is associated with the stranger, the fatherless and the widow). THOU SHALT NOT RESPECT PERSONS. There must be no evading of the law to please those in a high position (cp. 1.17). No bribes are to be taken.

THAT WHICH IS ALTOGETHER JUST SHALT THOU FOLLOW. The Hebrew repeats the word 'just'. S. R. Driver says: 'Justice, and only justice—justice without intermittence—is to be thy constant aim in judgment.' We must remember that, as Norman Snaith has said,[10] the word just or righteous 'means not only the establishment of righteousness    equal terms for all, but also the vindication by God of those who cannot secure their own rights.' He has also said:[11] 'For us, "justice" means either the demands of some moral law, or, more often, the King's justice. To the Hebrew it meant the demands of God's law, and God's justice.' But we must not let these two things

[10] *Distinctive ideas of the Old Testament*, p. 70.
[11] *op. cit.*, p. 74.

be separated. The basis of modern law is not justice but the will of the law-giver: but it is of urgent importance that law should not only be legal but also just. And man's understanding of the meaning of justice is cleansed, enriched and quickened by the worship of the living God.

## 16.21-22   No sacred poles or pillars allowed in worship
The words 'grove' and 'image' of the A.V., (Asherah and Matzebah in the Hebrew) are best translated 'pole' and 'pillar'. The Asherah was a pole or post planted in the ground near an altar (associated with a female goddess of that name); the Matzebah was a perpendicular stone pillar (associated with the masculine Baal). They were part of the normal setting of Canaanite worship, and indeed the worship of Israel before the Deuteronomic reform (cp. II Kings 13.6, 23.6-15; and Gen. 28.18-22, Ex. 24.4, Isa. 19.19).

The protest against them is not against their intrinsic significance, but against their associations—they have come to stand for a kind of worship incompatible with the worship of the true God. We see how details, which at one time were of no great significance, can come to have great importance, and their rejection or acceptance can be a determining issue of faith.

## 17.1   No unworthy sacrifice for God
No unworthy offering is to be made to God (cp. the later law in Lev. 22.17-25). There is a persistent temptation to be content with the second-best in religious life, which is dishonouring to God and degrading to the worshipper, and it must be resisted. The pressure of this temptation can be seen from Mal. 1.8.

## 17.2-7   The apostate (worshippers of the heavenly bodies) to be stoned
If any man or woman turns away from worshipping the true God to worship other gods—e.g. any one of the heavenly bodies—and if after enquiry this is proved, then he or she shall be stoned, first by the witnesses and then by all the people, and the evil put away from Israel.

The standard of evil is what is evil in the sight of God (cp. 4.25, 9.28, 31.29). Whatever the limitations in the application of this standard, it is fundamental that Deuteronomy is seeking to apply it. The impulse to worship the heavenly bodies has had a long history both before and long after this time. The Old Testament many times condemns it (cp. II Kings 17.6-7; 23.4-5 (Josiah's reformation), Jer. 8.2; 19.13; Ezek. 8.16).

The usual place for stoning was outside the city gate, as Stephen was stoned under the law (Acts 7.58). The law of witness is given in 19.15-21: here it is applied to see that the offence is proved. Though the sentence is carried out by all the people, the responsibility of the witnesses is shown by their taking the first act.

The writer to the Hebrews (10.26-31) refers to this passage in dealing with apostasy from the Christian Gospel and asks: 'Of how much sorer punishment, suppose ye shall be thought worthy, who hath trodden under foot the Son of God, and hath counted the blood of the Covenant, wherewith he was sanctified, an unholy thing, and hath done despite unto the Spirit of Grace?'

We shall have to consider this further on in relation to 32.35, which the epistle quotes to prove its point; we must say here that the writer is right in thinking that the repudiation of the Gospel is even more serious than the repudiation of the Old Covenant. But he is not right in accepting our present passage as wholly true to the mind of God in dealing with apostates.

This harsh repudiation of all false worship defeats its own end. It leads to an ignorant and oppressive conformity, and repudiates what may be at times a sincere, enlightened and creative non-conformity. The real problem of apostasy is the inward spirit, not the outward act, and that cannot be restrained by law. Even in a theocratic state the apostate needs caring for as a human being; in a community where the religious faith is not obligatory, the conquest of unbelief can only come from the vitality of positive faith.

# IV

## POSITIONS OF AUTHORITY
### 17.8-18.22

**17.8-13  No obedience to the decisions of the central court**
If a decision is too difficult for local decision it must be brought
to the central court. Such cases would be BETWEEN BLOOD
AND BLOOD, that is betwen accidental and wilful killing (cp. Ex.
21.12-14); BETWEEN PLEA AND PLEA, questions of property (cp.
Ex. 21.12-14), or BETWEEN STROKE AND STROKE, questions of
compensation for injuries (cp. Ex. 21.18-23). R. A. Knox is
vivid if inaccurate in his translation: 'Was it killing or was
it murder? Is this claim just or that? Was the infection
leprous or not?' The Bible in Basic English reads 'a decision
as to who is responsible for a death, or who is right in a cause,
or who gave the first blow in a fight?'

Adam Welch says:[1] 'What the code aims at bringing to an
end is the quarrelsomeness of the country village, where an
unsettled grievance can eat like a canker into the life of a
community and poison all wholesome relations among men
for more than one generation.'

The court is to be a mixed court of priests (on the priests,
the Levites, see 18.1) and judges as in 19.17 and 21.2-5, and
as in the court which the chronicler says that King Jehoshaphat
set up in Jerusalem (II Chron. 19.8-11).

In this section the word translated 'sentence' is simply
'word'; the word translated 'judgment' is the Hebrew word
*mishpat* and the word translated 'law' is the Hebrew word
*torah*. Norman Snaith says[2] of *mishpat* and *torah*: 'The two
words are synonymous to the extent that both are the declared
word of God. They are different in that *torah* at this early
stage meant an original pronouncement, while *mishpat* meant
a decision according to precedent.'

[1] *The Code of Deuteronomy*, pp. 93-4.
[2] *op. cit.*, p. 75.

107

The word *torah*—meaning direction rather than law—is
used elsewhere as a particular decision often on ceremonial
matters (cp. 33.10, Ezek. 22.26, Jer. 2.8, etc.); it is also applied
in a wider sense to mean the whole of the Deuteronomic covenant (see 1.5 and 17.18 and II Kings 10.31, 14.6, 17.13); and
again in a wider sense to mean the whole of the Pentateuch
(see Neh. 8.1-3, 13-14); finally it came to stand for the totality
of God's self-revelation.

A central court of justice must have power to enforce its
judgments. What is wrong with this law is that it makes death
the penalty and equates disobedience of the judgment of the
court with disobeying the God of Israel. The demand of God
must be definite if it is to exercise any controlling power in
human life; on the other hand, if it is tied too closely with the
decisions of any human institutions its absoluteness will be
brought into contempt. To act presumptuously against God is
not the same as dissenting from any human institution, however sacred.

### 17.14-20  The King must be loyal to God and his people
The law for the king belongs to Deuteronomy alone. It is born
of sad experience of the meaning of kingship in practice,
particularly in the Northern Kingdom from which it probably
comes. It is a warning to Israel that the King must acknowledge and fulfil his obligations to God and to his people. It is
a warning to the modern world that despotic power is incompatible with the acknowledgement of God and the well-being
of man.

The law says: if Israel sets up a king, he must be chosen by
God. He must not be like Solomon. He must be a student of
this law, and humble before God and his people. The law has
affinities with the later narrative of the institution of kingship
in I Sam. (7.2-17, 8, 10.17-27a, 12) which emphasized the dis-
advantages of having a king; rather than the earlier narrative
(9.1-10.16-27b, 11.1-11.15, 13, 14) which has no criticism whatever of the proposal to set up a king, no doubt seeing the
necessity of a king to guard the nation against external enemies
(cp. Judges 17.6, 21.25).

The king is to be chosen by God, as were Saul (I Sam. 10.24) and David (I Sam. 16.8-10, II Sam. 6.21). He is not to be a foreigner—a danger more possible in the Northern Kingdom and leading to a divided religious alliance.

The king is not to multiply horses, wives or wealth as Solomon did (I Kings 10.14-11.8). The prophets mention horses always in connection with foreign help and war (see Hos. 14.3, Isa. 2.7, Micah 5.10). The horse is for Israel first something they were unused to and unable to afford (cp. Josh. 11.9) and always the symbol of military power and aristocratic wealth. That the Messianic King is 'meek and lowly in heart' is emphasized by Zech. 9.9-10, which shows him riding upon an ass. This is endorsed in word and deed by Jesus (Luke 22.24-27, Mark 11.1-11, Matt. 21.1-11).

The phrase NOR CAUSE THE PEOPLE TO RETURN TO EGYPT (v. 16) may be a protest against the selling of Israelites as slaves into Egypt, but has a wider meaning, repudiating trading relations which might eventually lead to supplies of cavalry. This word of Yahweh is referred to again in 28.68. It is not known outside this book, but the same idea is expressed in Ex. 13.17, 14.13.

The king is to write a copy of this law from the one in charge of the priests. (The Hebrew word was misunderstood by the Greek translators to mean *this copy of the law* (*to deuteronomium touto*) from which the word Deuteronomy comes.) This is the beginning of that study and application of the written Word which has been so important a factor in Judaism and Christianity. Provided the evils of bondage to the letter are guarded against, the written word should be accepted with thanksgiving as the means of bringing later generations into intimate relation with the redeeming acts of God.

The king from his study of the law is to fear God and keep his laws and not to deal proudly and oppressively towards his fellow-countrymen from whom he has been chosen (compare Jeremiah's denunciation of Jehoiakim's unfair dealing with his workmen. Jer. 22.13-19).

The teaching of this law that the ruler of the people is under law to God, and that he has an obligation to deal righteously—

that is fairly and even generously—with them, is as necessary
to-day as it was then.

## 18.1-8   The support and equality of the priests, the Levites

       1-2   The priests, the Levites, depend on the offerings
       3-5   What is due to the priests
       6-8   A country priest coming to the central sanctuary
            shall share in the offerings

Before the time of Deuteronomy the priesthood was not defined
by any strict limits (see Ex. 4.4 and Judg. 17.7-13), and anyone
with priestly training was called a Levite. Here all Levites
are priests. In the later legislation a sharp division is made
between the sons of Aaron who are priests, and the Levites
who have inferior duties (see Lev. 8-10; Num. 3-4).

THE LORD IS THEIR INHERITANCE: that is, they have given
their whole time to the ministry of worship in Israel and must
be supported by the offerings made in worship. The principle
has been carried over into the Christian Church, e.g. St. Paul
says (I Cor. 9.14) 'Even so did the Lord ordain that they
which proclaim the Gospel should live of the Gospel', apparently relying on Luke 10.7 'for the labourer is worthy of his
hire'. A worthy and considerate but not luxurious provision
for the ministry is a test of the stability of any church. We
can see how the provision changed if we compare the present
passage with the earlier condition shown in I Sam. 2.12-17
and the later condition shown in Lev. 7.31-34.

Deuteronomy is concerned that all Israel shall be one fellowship, in which no one by misfortune or by wrongdoing shall
be unable to share if he has a right to be in the community. So it makes provision that the Levites who have
ministered in country districts, coming to the central sanctuary,
in full dedication of spirit shall be accorded full priestly rights
and privileges there. But it did not work out in practice.
Generosity of spirit which the worship of God inculcates does
not always make its clearest manifestations in religious
institutions. The country Levites were admitted to the fellowship, but not to the rights and privileges of the altar (II Kings
23.9).

In Ezek. 44.10-16 we have a justification of this setting aside of the Deuteronomic law, by a distinction between the Levites who were the sons of Zadok 'that kept the charge of my sanctuary when the children of Israel went astray from me' and the rest of the Levites who went astray from Israel and are only allowed to do the menial tasks of the Temple. The danger of ecclesiastical pride falsifying that consideration for others which is the product of faith and trust in God is always present. To meet it we can only watch and pray.

## 18.9-22 The contrast of prophecy with practices of magic and divination

        9-12 No divination in Israel
      13-14 Israel is to be perfect with God
      15-18 The true prophet is like Moses
      19-20 The true prophet is to be obeyed but the false prophet shall be put to death
      21-22 A word from God can be recognized because it comes true

The heart of the divine discipline of Israel is the training of Israel to look for God through the highest activities of human life and not through the lowest. Adam Welch says:[3] 'To Israel God was not Pan. He made and controlled all things, but His chief work was man. And when He told His will, He revealed it through His highest, not His lower, work.'

This means a turning away from the superstition that was so widely prevalent in the ancient world, and in more refined forms is not so far from the surface in the modern world.

The worst of these superstitions is the sacrifice of children in fire (cp. Lev. 18.21; II Kings 16.3 and 23.10 (Josiah's reformation)); the other eight are divining (cp. I Sam. 6.2, Ezek. 21.21); making strange sounds (cp. Lev. 19.26, Isa. 2.6); observing omens (cp. Lev. 19.26, Num. 23.23); practising sorcery (cp. Ex. 22.15, Jer 27.9); making spells (cp. Ps. 58.5, Isa.47); consulting the spirit of a dead person (cp. Lev. 19.31, I Sam. 27.3-14); having secret knowledge (cp. as before I Sam. 28.3-14); or seeking warning from the dead (cp. Isa. 8.19).

[3] *The Code of Deuteronomy*, p. 105.

(On all these forms of magic and divination see Alfred Guillaume: *Prophecy and Divination*. Bampton Lectures, 1938.)

George Adam Smith says: 'The sense of the incompatability of magic and necromancy with loyalty to the God of Israel is traceable from at least Saul's time onward, and is very articulate in the great prophets. The instinct was sound. That such practices divert men from the rational and ethical elements of religion and weaken both the judgment and will of those who resort to them is notorious in the history of modern spiritualism (cp. Luke 16.37, "If they hear not Moses and the prophets, neither will they be persuaded if one rise from the dead.") Let other nations hearken to soothsayers and diviners, God does not grant such to his people (v. 14). For them the living word of the living God is the thing.' (Isa. 8.19.)

The truth embodied in these prohibitions is that no true way to God involves attempting to escape the moral transformation which his word works in us. Attempts to find a neutral non-moral road inevitably lead to a weakening of moral character. We must not take this injunction as ruling out for the Christian the sphere of psychical research, but only as preventing us from attributing to psychical research what must come from our own response to God. And we must regret the too easy application of prejudice and suspicion to innocent people, and the harsh dealing with men and women guilty of these practices. Faith in the living God must win its way by the assent of the mind, not by the suppression of dissenters.

In v. 13 we have a verse which anticipates the word of Jesus in the Sermon on the Mount (Matt. v 48): 'Be ye therefore perfect, even as your Father which is in heaven is perfect.' The Hebrew word means 'blameless'. Israel in its walk before God is to be free from all the abominations that have been mentioned. And yet the word is one which lends itself to the widest interpretation. For what is perfection but life with God in freedom from all the distortions of humanity which others permit themselves?

But how is Israel to know God's will? Through his prophet, raised up from the midst of Israel. Israel had promised at

Horeb (5.27-28) to obey Moses speaking God's word to them and had been commended for it. God now promises to continue the prophetic witness, by raising a succession of prophets who shall speak in his name. That it is not one prophet only but a succession of prophets is not stated openly but is to be gathered from the context.

It was natural that Christian witness should turn to this passage and see in it a prediction of the coming of Jesus (cp. Acts 3.22, 7.37), and this is right if we think that this promise was fulfilled many times in Israel, but that its greatest and incomparable manifestation was in Jesus Christ our Lord. When we read, for example, in the Fourth Gospel (1.45) 'We have found him, of whom Moses and the law, and the prophets, did write'—the references may not be to this or any other passage, but to the cumulative testimony of the Old Testament.

Israel pledges obedience to the true prophet and death to the false prophet. Apart from the harsh treatment of those who may be religiously wrong, this is rightly the loyalty to which Deuteronomy calls Israel. Utter obedience to the true God, and utter rejection of what is contrary to his will. But in life it is not always easy to see where the issue lies. So long as we admit this, we need to be brought continually to the acceptance of this clear-cut division. A greater than the Deuteronomist said later, 'Ye cannot serve God and Mammon' (Matt. 6.24).

Israel is committed to obeying God, and its whole existence is bound up in doing so. We find in Jeremiah a confident expectation that he will be listened to because he is speaking a word from God (Jer. 26.12-15) and that disaster will befall Israel through not listening to the voice of God. This is true also in the New Testament. The apostle is an ambassador for Christ (II Cor. 5.20) and the Church is bound to listen and obey the truth of the Gospel (cp. Gal. 1.8).

We have seen in 13.1-5 that no prophecy can possibly be true which undermines the faith of Israel in the living God. But what positive test is there? Here we have added the test of effectiveness (cp. Jer. 23.22, 28.9). This answer does not

H

face the full inwardness of the problem of the truth of prophecy, because, while the word of God must prove its power of effective action it may not do so within the limits of time in which judgment must be made.

It was Jeremiah who did this, meeting in his own experience, the problem of non-fulfilment of prophecies uttered in obedience to God's call to him. Out of his own travail Jeremiah has made clear for all time the *context* in which the truth of prophecy is to be decided—the openness of the prophet to moral renewal, and the living reality of his personal communion with God.[4] But even Jeremiah did not solve the question, for the truth does not rest with the prophet himself, but whether in fact what he utters builds up the people of God in the fulness of their faith and life in him.

On this passage in Deuteronomy John Skinner comments:[5] 'The authors of the Deuteronomic legislation were aware of the dangers involved in the unrestrained exercise of freedom of prophesying; and in this attempt to regulate and control it, we have the first intimation of the radical opposition between the written code and the living voice of prophecy which ultimately led to the extinction of the latter.'

This is too harsh. We must also remember that the law is not in our sense a 'legal code', but 'preached law', and that this law is a law of promise. The prophet, of course, must be true to the inner witness of the Holy Spirit given to the Church as a whole. There is, unhappily, often conflict between the individual prophet and the Church as a whole in which the fault is sometimes on the one side and sometimes on the other. In the end they must come together, and the faith of the prophet be justified in the renewing of the faith of the whole Church.[6]

We must also note that the same issue arises in the New Testament. We must 'try the spirits, whether they are of God' (I John 4.1-6). The fundamental principle was laid down by St. Paul. 'No man speaking by the Spirit of God calleth Jesus accursed: and no man can say that Jesus is Lord, but

---

[4] cp. John Skinner, *Prophecy and Religion*, chap. x, Prophetic Inspiration.
[5] *op. cit.*, 1922. 1940 reprint, p. 190.
[6] cp. N. W. Porteous in *Record and Revelation*, 1938, pp. 235-6.

by the Holy Ghost' (I Cor. 12.3). C. H. Dodd[7] links I John
4.1-6 especially with Deut. 13.1-5 and says of Judaism and
Christianity: 'Both religions recognize the freedom of the
Spirit, and both owe something of their essential character to
its exercise. But both of necessity draw a line beyond which
such freedom is restrained by the demands of some fundamental truth.'

[7] *Commentary on the Johannine Epistles*, pp. 97-103.

# V

# LAWS MAINLY ON CRIME, WAR, PROPERTY, THE FAMILY
## 19.1-25.19

**19.1-13  The cities of refuge**
    1-3  Three cities for refuge
    4-7  For accidental killing
    8-10  If Israel grows, set apart three more cities
    11-13  No pity for the murderer

This, if we exclude the earlier reference in 4.41-43, is the Deuteronomic law on Cities of refuge. (The actual term is not found here, but comes later in Num. 35.11-12.) This law is an expansion and adaptation of the earlier law in Ex. 21.12-14 where the man who has killed by accident can flee to the nearest altar (Adam Welch has suggested that it is not the altar but a place of shelter or protection until due trial can be made).[1]

In the present law three cities are to be set apart for sheltering the man who has killed by accident. And if Israel grows in size, three more cities must be added, so that the cities are easy of access, but there is to be no pity for the wilful murderer. In the later law (to be found in Num. 35.9-34) there is elaboration of details by which the killing might be done; the benefits of the law are extended to cover the stranger and the sojourner; and the administration of justice transferred from the elders of a man's city to the high priest.

All these laws belong to an early state of society in which some restraint must be made upon blood-revenge, and the awareness of a distinction between different trends of killing has slowly come to expression. The term *avenger* (Hebrew *goel*) means the vindicator of a right and then redeemer. The Deuteronomist is well aware of the menace of the evil heart. In vv. 5-9 a practical duty is associated with the ultimate claim

[1] *The Code of Deuteronomy*, pp. 136-44.

of God—this mingling of the eternal and the temporal is the strength of Biblical faith.

The motive of the law is THAT INNOCENT BLOOD BE NOT SHED IN THY LAND, and this is a principle which can be carried far beyond the elementary expression given to it here. Just law always demands the protection of the innocent.

For wilful murder Hebrew law knows of nothing except death, here administered by the avenger of blood, with the elders of the city having judicial responsibility for handing the murderer over.

### 19.14  Boundary stones are not to be removed

Though this law on the removal of boundary stones is peculiar to Deuteronomy, the injunction not to remove them seems to have become proverbial in Israel (cp. 27.17; Hosea 5.10; Prov. 22.28; 23.10; Job 24.2). Many nations have put the established rights of property under religious sanctions. But religious sanctions cannot indefinitely prevent legitimate change.[2]

What this law fails to discriminate between is the protection of established rights against unjust dispossession, and the attempt to perpetuate economic conditions which have, in fact, passed away. In every time of change it is difficult to see the right application of religious and ethical standards, and the preacher is tempted to hark back to a time when distinctions were clear. But he is not always right. We must find a way to mix the absoluteness of religious standards with the acceptance of changing conditions, and combine a wise conservatism with a readiness to experiment in new ways.

### 19.15-21  No false witness in Israel

      15 Two witnesses necessary

      16-19 The false witness to receive what he would have inflicted

      20-21 The principle of retribution effective

The example given in 17.6 (cp. Num. 35.30) of the need of two witnesses to establish guilt, is here made into a general

---

[2] cp. the reference to enclosures in G. M. Trevelyan: *English Social History*, 1944.

rule, and has been accepted by civilized law. Only if one
man's word is checked by another can it be sufficient to condemn another man.

Honesty is the foundation of enduring social life: no man
must testify falsely against his brother with impunity. This
repudiation of false witness had to battle hard against that
perjury apparently endemic in Eastern countries; it was endorsed and reinforced by the teaching of Jesus (Matt. 5.33-37),
and needs re-emphasizing in public to-day. The Hebrew word
for 'false witness' is 'witness of violence'—a man who does
violence to the truth. Both men shall come before the central
court (see 17.9) and if the witness is found to be false, he shall
receive the punishment he would have inflicted upon his
brother.

This retribution will remove the evil from Israel. The principle shall be applied—LIFE SHALL GO FOR LIFE, EYE FOR EYE,
TOOTH FOR TOOTH, HAND FOR HAND, FOOT FOR FOOT (cp. Ex.
21.24-25, Lev. 24.18-20).

The law of equal retribution is not peculiar to the Old
Testament, but was widespread in the ancient world. It is
well to remember that it represents an advance on what went
before it. It puts an end to the interminable continuance of
blood-feud, each new requital starting a new act of retaliation,
and it put an end to the repayment of injuries with interest.
The law of equal retribution was in its turn limited in scope
by the principle of 24.16, that the responsibility of an individual was not shared by his group.

Deuteronomy thinks that its application will be effective,
Israel will fear, and the evil will be put away. We have learnt
in history that the effectiveness of the principle of retribution
can be exaggerated. It is not effective proportionately to the
heaviness of the punishment inflicted. Even equal retribution
is often more than is desirable or necessary to vindicate the
principle of retribution. Can it be dispensed with altogether
in favour of reformation? No. The principle of retribution
is necessary to the maintenance of the moral order. The
moral order, being sinned against, has a claim against the
offender. The acknowledgement of this in some form is

essential to true living. Beyond the acceptance of retribution
lies the possibility of reformation.

What, then, shall we say about Matt. 5.38-39? 'Ye have
heard that it hath been said, an eye for an eye and a tooth for
a tooth, but I say unto you that ye resist not evil: but whosoever shall smite thee on thy right cheek, turn to him the
other also.' This is a new standard, but it is a standard for
the morality of grace and not of law. It is a standard to
which individuals may rise, but which cannot be made the
basis of social life. Where particular persons commit themselves to this standard, then the possibilities of achievement
in the general life of the community rise too. But the need
for retribution in the life of the community remains still.

### 20.1-20  Laws to govern the practice of war

These laws to govern the practice of war are not found any-
where else. Adam Welch writes of them,[3] 'Everything is
here regarded, not from the point of view of practical warfare,
but from the point of view of religious dogma. Behind the
legislation lies the affirmation: " The Lord thy God walketh in
the midst of thy camp, to deliver thee, and to give up thine
enemies before thee " (23.14). Yahweh uses Israel as his instrument to do his work; and all for which Israel need provide
is to make itself a fitting instrument for this work. The
warriors, their camp, their methods of war, their uses of
victory, must be such as to satisfy Yahweh's claims; thereafter
he will give them victory '; and he adds, ' No doubt the Deuteronomists were a little ready, as in truth we are all a little
ready, to define the conditions which they counted necessary
for the full discharge of their divinely appointed duty, and to
take it for granted that what they believed to be thus necessary
must appear equally necessary to the Almighty.'

We ought not to exaggerate this. Religious faith in any
form appears to many people to be impracticable. And it
is certainly true that the ancient belief that true faith is the
determining factor in immediate practical success has been
shattered by hard fact. And yet concentration on immediate

[3] *The Religion of Israel under the Kingdom*, p. 222.

practicalities is not always the best way to deal with war or
with anything else.

**1-4** raise the question of the relation between faith in God
and war. The Christian is driven in two directions. Since
war can never be the direct expression of the Gospel, he has
a revulsion against it; but since war is one of the deepest
experiences in national life, he wants to speak the word of
God in the experience of war. The idea of the priest, speaking
in the name of God, bidding a nation be brave in its conflicts,
has not lost its meaning to-day.

In these battles, exemptions from service are allowed.
J. Pedersen[4] ascribed them to the need for 'maintaining that
state of increased psychic strength which is requisite in war'.
'In these three laws (i.e. vv. 5-7),' he writes, 'we find the same
considerate spirit which prevails in many of the laws of Deuteronomy, and which is generally characterized by the honourable
name "humane". A close inspection will show, however, that
the laws are not considering casual instances, but something
greater and more profound. In all three cases a man has started
a new important undertaking without having finished it yet.
In such a case something has been created which is greater
than the man himself, a new totality has come into existence.
To make a breach in this prematurely, that is to say, before it
has attained maturity or has been finished, involves a serious
risk of sin. This risk must be avoided for the sake of the
cause itself, and the man who came to the army after having
committed such a breach might mean a danger much more
than a help in the psychic whole constituted by the army.'

Perhaps some such conception underlies these exemptions,
but the point for us is that it operates in a humane direction.
(We may note that the service of God is different. From it
there are no exemptions. cp. Luke 9.57-62.)

The exemptions here concern marriage, home, work and
fear. The first three touch on the essential interests of human
life, whatever superstitious practices lie behind them. Fear
is a different matter. If men were exempted on account of
fear, how many would be left? We are here in the realm of

exhortation rather than law. George Adam Smith comments:
'The rule is in sympathy with this book's constant insistence
upon whole-hearted devotion in the service of God. In no
direction of life is he content with less.' We remember the
story of Gideon (Judg. 7.1-8). 'Fear is catching,' says Matthew
Henry, 'and in many an army is of most pernicious consequence.' Fear was even more important in ancient times
than to-day—as fighting seems to have been governed not by
elaborate strategy, but by impulses of flight or victory which
swept the whole army.

Before the first act of war, according to Deuteronomy, the
possibility of peace must be proclaimed. The tradition of the
Old Testament is in the direction, not of glorifying war, but
of rejoicing in peace. And yet the peace which is mentioned
here is the peace of submission. Peace is one of the great
words which are constantly liable to misuse, because we bend
them to suit our own desires.

The only outcome of war, according to Deuteronomy, is
victory—no doubt of this is remotely hinted. This perhaps
expresses the popular interpretation of the teaching of Isaiah
(cp. 33.1-6), but as Adam Welch says,[5] 'It needed the defeat
under Josiah at Megiddo, and the Exile to teach Israel and
especially the Deuteronomists that men have not to dictate to
their God the conditions of life which they count necessary, but
to accept those which He Himself lays down for them, and to
serve them there.'

In war, the law runs, all males are to be killed, though the
women and the little ones and the spoil are to be taken: but
the cities of the people whom Israel has displaced are to be
completely destroyed. This is the modified form of the *herem*
or ban (cp. 2.24-37, 13.12-18) by which through the destruction
of alien influences, Israel is to be kept loyal to the one true
God.

The fact that this is a theory invented long after the time
for dealing with Canaanite influences had passed has not prevented this law having a disastrous effect in history. If we
look at the chapter as a whole, we must notice the two-

[5] *The Religion of Israel under the Kingdom*, p. 223.

fold effect of religious faith on the practice of war. As George
Adam Smith says: 'In these laws of Deuteronomy religion
is seen sometimes mitigating and sometimes enhancing the
ferocity of war.'

This is a perpetual danger for religious people, and many
have welcomed a lessened public influence of religious faith in
the interests of peace and harmony. The absolute of faith in
God is necessary to give human life that depth and vitality
which is its promise and destiny. But if this absolute is mis-
placed, it is the source of suffering and great unhappiness. If
the faith which should be given to the one true God is released
upon aspects of human life, the result is a distorted energy
which, in the long run, is exhausting and unsatisfactory. If
the absolute is wrongly imposed upon matters which should
be left flexible, then life is given a harshness and rigidity
which takes a toll from human well-being.

The direction of the teaching of Deuteronomy is towards a
generous concern with human welfare. But, in desiring to
safeguard whole-hearted devotion to the one true God, it has
a strain of harshness and fanaticism. It is, however, much
easier to see this weakness of Deuteronomy, than to ensure
that our own religious faith shall not unwarrantably exacerbate
our human situation.

The chapter closes with an injunction to spare the fruit trees
in a siege. In v. 19 read: 'Is the tree of the field man that
it should be besieged of thee?' The destruction of fruit trees
was a practice in ancient warfare as we see from II Kings 3.19,
25. Israel may eat of the trees, but not cut them down,
because war is man's quarrel with man, not man's quarrel
with God's creation. This law is one which we need to take
account of in modern times, where the fury of destructive
power beggars the imagination. If man thinks himself at
liberty in war to destroy the common foundations of human
existence, then he is writing his own doom. We are all dependent upon the resources of God's creation, and the fertility
of the earth everywhere is the concern of every man.

In this chapter Deuteronomy has not risen to the height of
believing that all peoples belong to God and that war is

between nations who are all precious in the sight of God. On this question the book sheds no light.

The Christian, of course, must read this chapter and use it in conformity with allegiance to his overriding authority: the revelation of God in Jesus Christ. Christians are divided as to what this means.

'Three broad positions are maintained:

(1) There are those who hold that, even though entering war may be a Christian duty in particular circumstances, modern warfare, with its mass destruction, can never be an act of justice.

(2) In the absence of impartial supra-national institutions, there are those who hold that military action is the ultimate sanction of the rule of law, and that citizens must be distinctly taught again that it is their duty to defend the law by force if necessary.

(3) Others, again, refuse military service of all kinds, convinced that an absolute witness against war and for peace is for them the will of God and they desire that the Church should speak to the same effect.'[6]

In view of this, the Christian must seek the will of God in relation to possible and actual war, in the fellowship of the Church, remembering that others are doing the same, and rejoicing in the amount of agreement that does exist between all Christians on the fact of war; he must remember, under all circumstances, that all nations belong to God, and desire that the will of God for all nations shall come to pass in the earth; and he must care for his country and cherish her well-being (not necessarily success) and desire that she act in relation to the fact of war according to the highest moral standards available for moral action.

### 21.1-9  The removal of corporate guilt

This ancient law gives a ritual by which the corporate guilt, attaching to a community because of an untraced murder, may be removed from it. The function of the law in the Deuteronomic Code is to see that when this ritual is

[6] World Council of Churches Amsterdam Report, pp. 89-90.

performed, it is performed in the name of Yahweh the God
of Israel and not in the name of some other god. It is the
redeeming God of Israel to whom appeal is made, and the
standard of judgment is what is right in the sight of the Lord.

The responsibility is in the hands of the elders, with the
judges to assess where the liability lies and the Levites to
perform the ritual. The heifer, and the valley and the water
are not contaminated by common use. The symbolic action
of washing was believed to effect what it symbolized. We
remember that Pilate is said to have washed his hands to declare himself innocent of the blood of Jesus Christ (Matt. 27.24,
cp. Ps. 26.6, 73.13).

It is not by actions such as this that the corporate guilt of a
community can really be removed, but by sharing in the redemptive power of the living God expressed supremely in the
Cross of Christ that being transformed by the renewing of
their minds, they may prove what is that good and acceptable
and perfect will of God (Rom. 12.2).

### 21.10-14   A captured woman must be treated fairly
This section belongs to the Deuteronomic laws of war. The
view that a prisoner is the absolute property of his captor is
not directly denied, but limitations are placed on it. The
woman captive is to cleanse herself from her heathen impurities
and to be given time to mourn her separation from her own
home. If, after being taken as wife, she falls out of favour,
she must be set free. This law is one stage on the road to
the treatment of all persons—even prisoners of war—as
persons, not things. We cannot be said to have reached the
end of the road yet.

### 21.15-21   The rights and duties of sons
vv. 15-17 insist that the first-born son of a despised wife
shall be honoured. In the history of Israel, monogamy came
after long practice of other ways. And the distress and moral
evil of polygamy is exhibited to us in the literature. For
instances of a man having two wives see Gen. 29.16-30 (Jacob),
and I Sam. 1.1-2 (Elkanah). The first-born seems to have

inherited a double portion (cp. II Kings 2.9). As an instance
of this setting aside of the right of the first-born through the
influence of a favourite wife see I Kings 1-2 on Solomon's succession to the throne of David. In so far as the teaching of
this law is that in marriage we have accepted obligations which
we are not entitled to set aside at will, it still speaks to our
condition.

In vv. 18-21 the authority of the parents over a stubborn
and rebellious son is confirmed by the elders representing the
community (cp. 27.16). We must note that the mother is
linked in authority with the father as in the Ten Commandments. The earlier law in Ex. 21.15-17 gives absolute power
to the parents: here it is mitigated a little (cp. Lev. 20.9).
Gluttony and drunkenness are given as illustrations of rebellious conduct, not as an exhaustive list. The son is to be
stoned and the evil put away from Israel according to the
usual Deuteronomic formula (cp. 13.10-11; 17.5; 19.19-20).

One cannot help thinking that the attitude to parents is too
closely identified with the attitude to God. Compare Psalm
78.8 where the people are called 'a stubborn and rebellious
generation; a generation that set not their heart aright, and
whose spirit was not steadfast with God'. The problem of
the revolt of sons against parents has persisted down the
centuries. Stoning is a harsh and repellent method of dealing
with it. It is only fair to say that we know nothing about its
being practised. In Proverbs 30.17 it is suggested that disobedience to parents will lead to disaster but not to legal
punishment.

## 21.22-23  The hanged is accursed

The body of a criminal was hanged after death as a mark
of dishonour (see Josh. 8.29-10.26; I Sam. 31.10—II Sam.
4.22). It must be buried the same day so that the promised
land should not be defiled (cp. Gen. 4.11; Num. 35.33-4).

It is not unnatural that the earliest Christians should reflect
upon this verse. Crucifixion was not what was meant, but it
was inevitable that the meaning should be extended. The
bodies of the crucified were taken down the same day because

of the Sabbath (John 19.30). There are two references in
Acts to the hanging of Jesus upon a tree (5.30; 10.39).

St. Paul boldly claims the word as a word of promise (Gal.
3.13). 'Christ hath redeemed us from the curse of the law,
being made a curse for us: for it is written Cursed is every
one that hangeth on a tree.' He does not quote here the words
'of God', but this must not be taken as weakening the effect
of the words—the curse of the law was part of God's plan
for dealing with evil. He does not explain in what way
Christ has become a curse for us, but simply asserts that
Christ in his identification with humanity in its lowest point
has opened a way of new life for us all beyond the curse of
the law. The linking of the passage (Gal. 3.10-14) with this
verse is in a sense arbitrary as it is not relevant to the primary
meaning of the injunction in Deuteronomy: but for the Christian understanding of the whole meaning of the curse in
Deuteronomy the passage is very relevant.

### 22.1-4   Neighbourliness
If a man sees his brother's ox or sheep go astray, he shall
not pretend that he has not noticed, but shall bring them to
their owner or shall look after them till he can find them. And
so with a lost ass, or lost clothing, or anything else. And if
a man sees an animal in difficulties he shall help to raise it.

The injunction is a rephrasing of the older law in Ex. 23.4-5
which speaks of 'thine enemy's ox' and 'the ass of him that
hateth thee'. This seems a more direct anticipation of Matt.
5.44, 'Love your enemies', than the Deuteronomic form. But
it is not intended to limit the requirement of neighbourliness
since the comprehensive term 'brother' is used, and the demand is that neighbourliness shall have a claim overriding
all personal feeling of dislike or estrangement.

Matthew Henry says on v. 4, 'This must be done, both in
compassion to the brute creatures, for *a merciful man regardeth
the life of a beast* (Prov. 12.10), though it be not his own, and
in love and friendship to our neighbour, not knowing how
soon we may have occasion for his help. If one member may
say to another "I have at present no need of thee", it cannot

say " I never shall ".' But the injunction goes beyond this—we are exhorted to help another because he is in need, and because we ought to care for his interests. The principle of neighbourliness is that we are our brother's keeper.

The deepest word in the passage is the command not to hide ourselves from our brother's need (v. 3). We realize, then, that the priest and the Levite in the parable of the Good Samaritan (Luke 10.31-32) were acting against the spirit of Old Testament teaching.

## 22.5   Do not wear the clothes of the other sex

This custom is directed against customs of non-Israelite worship. It has no direct implication for modern life. We may, however, note that the sharp distinction between male and female characteristic of Judaism is not characteristic of the Christian Church (cp. Gal. 3.28), 'there is neither male nor female: for ye are all one in Christ Jesus'. But the recognition of the relative difference of the sexes within their common unity as persons needs safeguarding.

## 22.6-7   Spare the mother bird

The motives suggested for this injunction are: (a) kindness to living creatures (cp. 22.1-4, 25.4, Luke 12.6); (b) reverence for motherhood with the same promise as in the fifth commandment (v. 16); (c) the right of use in the bird which remains common property. In any case, it is a restriction upon liberty of action for the sake of general well-being.

## 22.8   Make your roofs safe

While there is the thought of the sharing of the house in the taint of innocent blood spilt, the purpose of the law is care for human life. The roof of an eastern house was flat or oval, and was used for conversation, fresh air, and worship. Without a parapet it was not safe. This use of a roof is mentioned, for example, in Josh. 2.6 (Rahab), Judg. 16.27 (The Philistines and Samson), II Sam. 11.2 (David and Bethsheba), Acts 10.9 (Peter at Joppa). For its use as a place of worship see

Neh. 8.16, Jer. 19.13, Zeph. 1.5. We have no excuse for want of thought or carelessness where other people's lives are at stake.

## 22.9-11  No mixing

Mixtures of seed, animals for ploughing, and material are forbidden. The first and third of these are given also in Lev. 19.19: the reason for the first, and mention of the second are given here only. Matthew Henry comments: 'There appears not any thing at all of moral evil in these things, and therefore we now make no consequence of sowing wheat and rye together, ploughing with horses and oxen together, and wearing linsey-woolsey garments, but hereby is forbidden either (1) a conformity to some idolatrous customs of the heathen; or (2) that which is contrary to the plainness and purity of an Israelite.'

## 22.12  Tassels

Plaited tassels are to be worn at the four corners of the outer garment which is mentioned in 24.13. The later law in Num. 15.37-41 gives a reason for this: 'that ye may look upon it and remember all the commandments of the Lord and do them'. It is these tassels which are referred to when we are told of the woman with an issue of blood touching the hem of the garment of Jesus (Matt. 9.20, Luke 8.44); other sick people also thronged to touch them (Mark 6.56, Matt. 14.36). The Christian Church decided at an early period in its history that it was not bound by this kind of regulation (Acts 15).

## 22.13-30  Sexual Standards

The laws in this section, together with 24.1-4, 25.5-9, constitute the teaching of Deuteronomy on the marriage relationship. The only law on the subject earlier than these in the Old Testament is in Ex. 22.16-17 (except as regards female slaves, Ex. 21.7-11) roughly corresponding to vv. 28-29, but providing for the recompense of the father if he does not want his daughter to marry the man who has had intercourse with her.

The laws here deal with *virginity*. If a man accuses his wife of lack of virginity he shall produce proof now known to be crude and uncertain. If the test goes in her favour, the man shall be fined; if it goes against her she shall be stoned.

*Adultery* shall be punished with death for both the man and the woman. This law is endorsed by Lev. 20.10.

*Engagement* is treated as a binding pledge of the same order as that of marriage. If there is sexual intercourse with an engaged girl, with her consent, the punishment shall be as for adultery. If without, the man only shall die.

If a man has sexual relations with an unattached girl, he shall pay her father a bride-price and have no right of divorce.

An inheriting son may not marry his stepmother or have sexual intercourse with any of his father's wives. This is endorsed in 27.20 and in Lev. 18.8, 20.11. This is the first instance of laws of prohibited degrees or relationship in marriage which are developed in Lev. 18. For the offence against which the law protests see II Sam. 16.22.

From a historical point of view these laws deserve considerable respect as part of the pressure away from a state of polygamy to a state of faithful monogamy. When we consider their permanent validity, we are bound to shrink from the Deuteronomist's method of putting away evil. The sexual side of community life is so important that drastic measures must be taken to ensure purity and punishment. If, in the modern world, we recognize that there is not always so simple a solution of sexual problems, we do well to remember that our margin of flexibility is not unlimited. Purity and fidelity are still essential and still have to be secured.

While these laws bring the main offender sternly to task, they do not treat women fully as persons having an adequate status which must be taken fully into account. They helped rather than hindered that goal, but in themselves they do not embody it. The emancipating effect of the attitude of Jesus to woman was very great indeed.

Over the marriage laws of Israel, is the concern that Israel in its human relationships shall act worthily of Israel's God. And the conviction of Israel is, that because God is faithful and under all circumstances we can trust him, he will help his

I

people to overcome the human unfaithfulness which these laws prohibit.

### 23.1-8 Those excluded from the Church of Israel

In this law the purity of Israel's religious assembly is safe-guarded. The word translated ' congregation ' in the A.V. is the word *Qahal* which probably became the word *ekklesia*, church, of the New Testament. Here are the exclusions from the religious community of Israel. On what grounds are they made? Physical imperfection (which may have had hostile religious associations) and historic descent. It is to be noted that in the New Testament, apart from betrayal of the stan-dards of the Christian community, exclusion depends on the will of the person. Whosoever will, let him take of the water of life freely (Rev. 22.17).

**1.** There are to be no eunuchs in the Church of Israel (cp. Lev. 21.20). The mutilations referred to are probably con-cerned with alien religious rites. In contrast to this Isa. 56.1-8 in a passage leading up to the declaration: ' mine house shall be called a house of prayer for all people', God promises to eunuchs who keep his sabbaths an everlasting Name. In Acts 8.26-40 we have the story of the reception of a eunuch into the infant Christian Church. (The teaching of Jesus in Matt. 19.12 refers on the one hand to physical conditions, and on the other to those who, for the sake of the Kingdom, have given up the possibilities of marriage.)

**2.** There are also to be no bastards in Israel to the tenth generation that is, for ever. By these are meant products of incestuous unions, as indeed Ammon and Moab (v. 3) were popularly supposed to be (cp. Gen. 19.30-38). v. 4. The earlier account in this book (2.16-29) does not criticize Ammon and Moab for their unfaithfulness to Israel: indeed, v. 29 directly denies it. For the hostility between these peoples and Israel see Amos 1.13, Zeph. 2.8, Isa. 16.6.

He—not they as A.V.—that is, Moab, hired Balaam. For the story of Balaam see Num. 22-24. Balaam had a bad name in Jewish thinking probably from the influence of the later passage in Num. 31.8-16, according to which he was responsible for immoral influences in Israel. This was accepted by early Christian writers (see II Peter 2.15, Jude 11, Rev. 2.14). Afterwards Jewish writers thought of Balaam as the type of the false prophet and some even applied his name to our Lord. Of the character in the original composite story in Num. 22-24, Walter Lock speaks of[7] 'the half-conscious Gentile soothsayer' who is 'a warning especially to the preacher that no beauty of utterance, however flawlessly beautiful, no heralding of truth to others however unqualifiedly true, is sufficient to prevent a man being himself a castaway'. The reference here, while derogatory to Balaam, with its suggestion of prophesying to order, is right in seeing in the story a vindication of the power of the God of Israel to turn curse into blessing.

**3-5** are used to justify the action of Nehemiah in Neh. 13.1. Israel is commanded (v. 6) not to seek the peace and prosperity of Ammon and Moab. The idea is repeated in Ezra 9.12, but in Jer. 29.7 Israel is taught to pray for the peace of Babylon. Deuteronomy is concerned that Israel shall really be a considerate brotherhood. This implies for the author lack of concern for those outside. Not until we realize that there are none outside the range of God's Kingdom can the full power of the positive message of Deuteronomy be fulfilled. All people are God's people (cp. Ps. 24.1).

**7-8.** The Edomite and the Egyptian, however, belong to the Church of Israel in the third generation (cp. 2.4 and Isa. 19.18-25). An instance seems to be mentioned in Jer. 36.14. Even in Deuteronomy with its hostility to alien corrupting influences, there is some concern to bring others in to the redemptive power of Israel's God.

### 23.9-14   The Holiness of the Camp
This primitive ritual belonging to the laws of war is brought under allegiance to the God of Israel. In ancient times everything sexual was mysterious and, if not properly dealt with, exposed to peril. The motive behind this law is religious, but the sanitary effect would help its perpetuation. At the same

[7] *Journal of Theological Studies*, ii, 161-73.

time the lesson that 'cleanliness is next to godliness' is a lesson religious people have been slow to learn.

The important thing here is the motive. THE LORD THY GOD WALKETH IN THE MIDST OF THE CAMP. God is in the midst of his people, and therefore the whole of life, in its degree, must be lived in a way that is fit for the presence of God. Where this is steadily adhered to, the distortions and corruptions of human life will disappear.

### 23.15-16   Israel a refuge for escaped slaves

In contrast with the existing practice (see I Kings 2.39-40) this law affirms that slaves who escape into Israel shall not be given back, and shall not be oppressed. Freedom from alien wills is native to the human spirit in the purpose of God, but men have been slow to recognize it. It is characteristic of Deuteronomy to think of God's people as the friends of freedom.

### 23.17-18   No sexual licence in worship

Sex is so central a fact in human life that it is not unnatural that human beings have sought to use it in their approach to God. But it is characteristic of the greatness of the faith of Israel to repudiate this. Whatever the preciousness of sex in faithful human love, it is not in and by itself alone a means of approach to God. The use of sex in worship, in itself, and in fulfilment of a pledge, degrades the Name of the God who is worshipped and also those who worship.

Our customs are different from the ancient world, but we are still in danger of over-valuing and under-valuing sexual experience. The supreme moment of experience is not the act of sex, whatever its enriching function in marriage, but rather the transformation of mind and heart in love and obedience to God.

### 23.19-20   Interest on loans allowed from foreigners only

The passage prohibits interest from loans (given probably to meet cases of personal need) from fellow Israelites, while allowing it either in such cases or in commercial loans from

foreigners. The term 'usury' found in the A.V. is simply
the old word for 'interest', and does not imply excessive interest. In this generalized form, the injunction is an advance
upon the two parallel laws in Ex. 22.25 and Lev. 25.37, which
forbids taking interest from poor Israelites. Here the prohibition is extended to all *Israelites*.

This prohibition is in line with the general sentiment of
Greek and Roman moral teachers. This may be due to a
cultural contempt for trade, and it is not clear whether such
prohibitions affected commercial dealings. The taking of
interest is mentioned in Matt. 25.27 as a normal fact, without
condemnation.

Adam Welch sees in this law [8] an attempt 'at social legislation which represented a conservative reaction and an effort
to preserve conditions which were passing away . . . So
soon as men wanted money on loan, not in order to enable
them to fulfil their duties to the community, but in order to
make more money with it, the situation as between debtor
and creditor was put outside the old relations . . . What
preserved the Deuteronomic legislation from becoming a mere
conservative reaction was that it recognized the unity of the
nation in its traditions of God's grace, in its common worship
of him who was still gracious, and in the mutual duties which
sprang out of these.'

And Dr. Welch comments: [9] 'It is an interesting parallel to
note how when the industrial revolution took place in Britain
which altered the old relations in which masters and servants
had stood, men like Ruskin and Carlyle turned to glorify the
old order which had a moral basis they could understand, and
shrank from the new order which had not yet evolved the moral
basis without which they recognized that it could prove little
beyond confusion.'

It is an ironical turn of history, if injunctions, which were
out of date when promulgated, have been used in later centuries
to try and stem the flood of entirely new conditions with
authoritative moral commands. The permanent meaning of

[8] *The Religion of Israel under the Kingdom*, pp. 228-31.
[9] *op. cit.*, p. 291.

these verses lies not here, but in the concern that those in need
should not be exploited.

### 23.21-23  Keep your word
It has been mentioned in 12.6, 11, 17, 26 that vows are to be
paid at the central sanctuary. Here it is said that while a man
is free to vow or not to vow, once he has given his word he
must keep it. This is supported, not denied, by Matt. 5.33-37,
which reinforces Deuteronomy's plea for honesty of intention
and execution (as against that false promise prohibited in the
third commandment by the Decalogue 5.11). In the Pentateuch the Deuteronomic law is endorsed in Num. 30.2 in a
chapter which is an elaborate discussion of women's vows.

The two limitations on the keeping of our word—that circumstances have entirely changed, and that our vow commits
us to something that runs counter to our moral conviction—
are not mentioned here: but the difficulty meets us in one of
the famous stories of the Old Testament, that of Jepthah—to
offer whatever came out of his house to meet him, and it was
his daughter (Judg. 11.30-31). This story probably has its
origin in a fertility rite, and as it stands it is a deliberate act
and not a rash unthinking commitment. But it has been
accepted as a classical instance of the wrong sort of vow.

### 23.24-25  Use of a neighbour's crops to satisfy hunger
The practice of generosity instead of greediness is the means
of true fellowship in a community. The owner of a vineyard
or a cornfield ought not to demand the last ounce of it for himself; neighbours ought not to trespass on his hospitality by
taking more than will satisfy their hunger. Jesus protested
against later refinements in this law which nullified its meaning, asserting that the authority of his ministry is greater even
than that of the law (Mark 2.23-28; Matt. 12.1-8; Luke 6.1-5).

### 24.1-4  A man cannot remarry his divorced wife
No Hebrew law institutes divorce. The fact has already been
mentioned in 22.19, 28, where the possibility of divorce is
removed by misconduct. Mal. 2.13-16 makes clear the preva-

lence of divorce and God's hatred of it. The other laws in
the Pentateuch deal with the situation of divorced women (Lev.
21.7, 14, 22.13, Num. 30.9).

No man can remarry his divorced wife who has married
again, because the covenant of exclusive allegiance is defiled
through the relationship into which she has entered with the
other man. The law is aimed at preventing the easy passage
of a woman from one man to another, and is therefore in the
interests of the woman. The provision that, if divorce takes
place because of unfitting behaviour, a bill of divorcement
shall be given her, before she is dismissed, is in her interest.

The story of Hosea (1-3) is the story of a man who refuses
to divorce his wife, however unfaithful she has been. So God
is faithful to Israel, whatever her unfaithfulness. This teaching is carried on, repudiating the possibility of a divorce
between God and Israel in Isa. 1.1-3; Jer. 3.1-8.

In the Gospels (Mark 10.1-12, Matt. 5.31-32, 19.1-12, Luke
16.18) Jesus establishes complete equality between man and
woman; makes clear that the admission of the possibility of
divorce is a concession to the hardness of men's hearts; and
reaffirms the aim of marriage as given in Gen. 1.27, 2.24 as
lifelong fidelity between one man and one woman—a union
whose claims are superior even to those of parents.

We owe to the Hebraic tradition, slowly making its essential character clear, as reinforced and cleansed by Jesus Christ,
a true picture of the claims and possibilities of marriage. We
cannot afford to let it be destroyed in the modern world.

### 24.5 Exemption of the newly-married
We have seen already that the newly-married man is to be
exempt from service in war (20.7). Here he is also excused from
public office. For CHEER HIS WIFE read 'enjoy himself with
his wife'.

### 24.6 A mill or upper millstone must not be taken in pledge
The word translated in the A.V. the 'nether millstone' is the
mill itself. The 'upper millstone' is the lighter and more easily
moved stone. The law is a law against taking any man's liveli-

hood away from him.   Under all circumstances a man must
be left self-respect and independence.

Matthew Henry writes: 'Consonant to this is the ancient
common law of England which provides: That no man be
distrained of the utensils and instruments of his trade or
profession, as the axe of a carpenter, or the books of a scholar,
or beasts belonging to the plough, as long as there are other
beasts, of which distress may be made (Coke I, Inst. fol. 47).
This teaches us to consult the comfort and subsistence of others
as well as our own advantage.   That creditor who cares not
though his debtor and his family starve, nor is at all concerned
what becomes of them so he may get his money or secure it,
goes contrary, not only to the law of Christ, but even to the
law of Moses too.'

### 24.7   No Israelite can sell another as a slave

This law is adapted from Ex. 21.16 to make clear that Israel
is a brotherhood and that men must act considerately towards
all who share the same corporate life.

### 24.8-9   Precautions against leprosy

Leprosy in the Bible covers a number of skin diseases including
true leprosy.   The later law in Lev. 13-14 is a detailed instruction to be given by the priests; here we have a general statement for the ordinary Israelite, asking for obedience to the
instruction (torah) of the priests—the Levites. We are reminded
of the story of Miriam which is preserved for us in Num. 12.
There it is recorded that God smote her with leprosy (cp. II
Kings 5.27, 15.5) for belittling the uniqueness of Moses.   In
the Gospels Jesus shows himself willing to touch a leper
(Mark 1.41), but in healing the lepers asks them to conform
to the instructions of the priests (Luke 17.14).

The law reminds us of the slowness with which medical
science gained a true independence of religious control: we
may to-day need to emphasize that religious faith too has a
part to play in combating disease.   What happened in the incident of Miriam we cannot say: perhaps the story finds a
reason for the fact that she was stricken with leprosy, and uses

the incident to indicate the position and authority of Moses. It is important that we shall see the judging action of God in the midst of life: but it is also dangerous. It is particularly dangerous when we use the term to suppress any criticism of those in authority.

### 24.10-13   On taking and restoring pledges

Of these two laws about pledges, the first one peculiar to Deuteronomy enjoins that the privacy of a man's house shall be respected. The second follows the law of Ex. 22.26-27, and says that if a man pledges his outer cloak it must be returned at sunset so that he may sleep in it. The clothing referred to is 'the largest and heaviest article of Oriental dress, being the dress of travel of the shepherd, worn for protection against cold and rain, and used as a covering against sleep'.[10] This kind of activity will stand to a person's credit with God. It is in fact action akin to that in which God manifests his saving righteousness.

Both these laws are concerned with protecting the possibility of the fullest sharing by every person in the community life. Whatever the poverty of fellow Israelites, their right to a place where they are free to act for themselves, and their right not to be deprived of elementary necessities must be respected. Any other standard of action destroys the moral basis of community life. To apply those laws in the complexity of modern life is difficult, but the principle underlying them is just as true in modern life as in ancient.

### 24.14-15   Earned money not to be withheld from those who need it

The day labourer, whether he is Israelite or stranger, shall be paid on the day of his work. The law is repeated in Lev. 19.13. It is used in the denunciations of the rich in James 5.4, where the word 'oppress' becomes 'defraud'.

Those who have to live from hand to mouth are at the mercy of those who exploit them. Often we suffer from a defect of imagination about the financial situation of other people,

[10] Hastings *Dictionary of the Bible*, i, 625.

which we imagine to be like our own. A generous imaginative
insight into the living conditions of other people is essential to
social well-being. But where there is imagination it may be
used ungenerously to exploit the very need of other people in
the interest of the stronger. This is contrary to the will of
God, and Deuteronomy, by insisting on the payment of the
day labourer on the day of his work, repudiates the exploita-
tion of the poor.

### 24.16  No corporate punishment for individual crime

In Israel and in other ancient peoples corporate responsibility for individual wrongdoing was attributed to the family
or group (cp. Josh. 7.1-26, II Sam. 21.1-9, Esth. 9.12-19).
Amaziah, King of Judah (796-789), broke with custom in not
slaying the families of those who murdered his father (II Kings
14.1-7). His justification, according to the compiler of the
Book of Kings, lay in this Deuteronomic law, but it is probable
that Amaziah's act made the law possible. This law, which
limits the law of equal retribution (19.21) to the person concerned, paved the way for the teaching of Jeremiah (see
particularly 31.29-34) and Ezekiel on individual responsibility
(see particularly 18.1-32).

This law is not in conflict with the reason given for the
second commandment (v. 9), because God's visitation there
is the inevitable consequence of human solidarity, not special
action which calls for imitation.

We should have said that the lesson of this law had been
learnt once for all, were it not that we have seen in the twentieth
century whole communities punished for individual wrongdoing. We must continually re-learn the lessons of God's
people.

The recognition of individual responsibility does not repudiate the solidarity of the brotherhood of Israel: rather, it
paves the way for a richer expression of it. The community
is rich in the individuals it nourishes, and the individual is
rich as he receives from and gives to the community. C. H.
Dodd says,[11] ' It would be untrue and misleading to suggest

[11] *The Bible To-day*, p. 147.

that the New Testament represents the culmination of a development in the direction of individualism. It is of course true that the religious and moral significance of the individual is asserted by New Testament writers at least as firmly as by Jeremiah; but on the other hand the conception of an organic solidarity of the people of God reaches its fullest expression in the New Testament idea of the Church as the " Body of Christ ".'

### 24.17-22  Generosity to the weak

The stranger, the fatherless and the widow are the special concern of the Deuteronomist. And this concern is bound up with his sense of the determinative character of the crucial experience of Israel's history. At the centre of Israel's life is the experience of being dealt generously with by the living God. This is the characteristic experience which is renewed in worship. Out of this experience must come conduct which is equally characteristic—the generous dealing with the weak and helpless.

In vv. 17-18 we have the insistence that justice must be done to those who out of their own strength cannot insist upon it. In vv. 19-22 neither harvest nor olive trees nor vineyard must be drained of their fruits. Something must be left over for those who need it to gather. Similar laws are to be found in Ex. 22.21-22, 23.6-9 and Lev. 19.33. The second law is developed in Lev. 19.9-10 which deliberately leaves the corners to be gleaned.

### 25.1-3  The limit which punishment must not exceed

When after full trial, a man is found guilty and ordered to be beaten, the number of strokes he is to be given must be limited and given in the presence of the judge. Forty stripes is the maximum number. It must not be exceeded: to do this is to bring the offender into contempt.

' The need for insisting on a full trial,' says George Adam Smith, 'is seen from Jer. 20.2, 37.15 (cp. Acts 16.22-23, 37), as these show beating or scourging was apt to be given (even by the Romans) on arrest.' S. R. Driver comments on this law that it is 'a provision both equitable and necessary in an age when little regard was apt to be paid to human suffering, and when corporal punishment was liable to be inflicted with extreme severity'.

The distinctive word in the law is 'lest, if he should exceed, then thy brother should seem vile unto thee'. The personality of the offender must be respected even in punishment. The criminal law must not harm either judge, by causing him to indulge in contempt of his brother, or criminal, by causing him to lose that self-respect which is the foundation of his humanity.

We are familiar from II Cor. 11.24 with the fact that punishment was in fact limited to thirty-nine stripes, in order that the law should not be transgressed by accident, and the administrator punished for misdemeanour.

The principle that punishment should be limited to the least possible compatible with the vindication of the claim of just law to obedience is of great importance and permanent application.

### 25.4   Kindness to the working ox
The ox, who is due to share in the rest of the sabbath (v. 14), shall be given freedom to do his work happily and well. The verse is quoted by St. Paul in I Cor. 9.9 to reinforce his plea that the ministry is entitled to adequate financial support (his teaching here is repeated in I Tim. 5.18). He impatiently sweeps away the literal meaning in order to insist on that wider application which has support in the teaching of Jesus (Matt. 4.4, 22.29-33). But the literal meaning is still there and important. Those who acknowledge God will show consideration for the living creatures who serve them.

### 25.5-10   Marriage with the widow of a dead brother
If a man die childless, a brother living in the same house shall marry his widow to give his brother a son. If he will not do this, he shall be publicly condemned. Such a marriage (called levirate marriage from the Latin *levir*, husband's brother) is a primitive custom to perpetuate the name of a

man. See Gen. 28.8. The story of Ruth and Boaz (Ruth 4.1-12) is similar, but based on a wider relationship. The custom was probably growing obsolete when Deuteronomy was written. It also (cp. 24.1-4) is a concession to the hardness of men's hearts, who look to physical continuity rather than personal relationship. In the later laws ordinary marriage with a brother's wife is forbidden (Lev. 18.16; 20.21), and inheritance by daughters allowed (Num. 27.7-8). The latter partly does away with the purpose of this law.

The Sadducees used this law to try and prove the absurdity of the belief in the resurrection (Mark 12.18-27; Matt. 22.23-33; Luke 20.27-38). Jesus says that the resurrection is not simply a prolongation of human marriage arrangements, but the entering upon a new order of life. 'In the resurrection they neither marry nor are given in marriage, but are as the angels of God in heaven.'

### 25.11-12 Immodest Assault
This law is a primitive one penalizing a woman for breach of the taboo attaching to the sexual organs. It is the only instance of mutilation prescribed by Deuteronomy, apart from the law of equal retribution (19.21). Matthew Henry says: 'Modesty is the hedge of chastity, and therefore ought to be very carefully preserved and kept up by both sexes.'

### 25.13-16 Honesty in Trade
No Israelite is to have among his property, weights and measures which represent different standards. The use of false standards is unjust and hateful to God; whereas the use of true weights and measures will bring prosperity and long life in the promised land.

A parallel law is to be found in Lev. 19.35-36, and in Ezek. 45.10; just balances are demanded. Amos 8.5 denounces the iniquity of different standards for buying and selling; and Micah 6.10 repudiates the scant measure. In Prov. 16.11 this has become generally accepted.

W. A. L. Elmslie says:[12] 'The vitality in Hebrew religion

[12] *How came our Faith*, pp. 6-7.

was due to the impact made on the nation's intelligence and conscience by men whose genius it was to believe that morality is not the title of a haphazard game without rules, in which one opinion is as good as another. They held that certain qualities are *really* right, and others *really* perversion of what men should be. Effort to discriminate Right from Wrong is not pursuing a will-o'-the-wisp illusion, because Ultimate Reality (God) is Absolute Goodness.'

Honest dealing is rightly to be expected from those who believe in God, and belief in the living God is an urgent constraint to deal honestly with men.

### 25.17-19 Amalek

Ex. 17.8-16 in a striking passage had already declared God's purpose to 'put out the remembrance of Amalek from under heaven'. This is repeated here with a more illuminating reason for Israel's hatred—the persistent cruelty of Amalek to the stragglers in the wilderness. This hatred persisted in Israel's history (I Sam. 14.48; 15.1-31; 27.8-9; 31.20; II Sam. 8.12). By the time Deuteronomy was written the Amalekites had probably disappeared from history.

It is ironical that the memory of Amalek should be preserved in the religious traditions of Israel. A persisting grudge, whatever the provocation for it, is not a pretty thing. The mind must be cleansed from it by the power of that forgiveness which had so distinctive a place in the New Testament (cp. Matt. 18.22).

# VI

# TWO FORMS OF SERVICE FOR THE WORSHIP OF THE GOD OF ISRAEL
## 26.1-15

### 26.1-11   Thanksgiving to God for the Promised Land

These two forms of service express the characteristic concern of the Deuteronomist that the worship of Israel shall be given to Yahweh the God of Israel and to no one else. The name of God in various forms occurs nine times in this section. The land of Israel is the gift of God to his people, as he promised. Thanksgiving must be made to him and to no one else.

Every year the Israelite must acknowledge that the land he lives in is the Promised Land which Yahweh the God of Israel swore to his fathers to give him (see 1.8 and Gen. 12.7, 26.3, 28.13), by offering to the true God at the prescribed altar a basketful of first-fruits. (The first-fruits have been mentioned already as the due of the priests.)

The Israelite must make his acknowledgement before the priest in order to ensure that the worship is really paid to the true God and to him alone. And he must acknowledge first, that this is the Promised Land of God's gift, and second, that it is by God's redemptive act that he is able to share in it. The story starts from Jacob, a nomad Aramaean (A.V. 'A Syrian ready to perish') whose mother, Rebekah, was from Aram-Naharaim (Gen. 24.10 R.V. marg., cp. Gen. 24.4), and he himself was a shepherd in Aram (Hos. 12.12, Gen. 29-31) and had Aramaean mothers to his children. He went down into Egypt with a small company—traditionally seventy (cp. 10.22, Gen. 46.26-27). This people was oppressed by the Egyptians, and cried unto Yahweh, the God of their fathers, and he delivered them and brought them into the Promised Land. The story has not been told in Deuteronomy, where it is presupposed and the details are borrowed from the older

account (cp. Ex. 1.12, 14; 2.23; 3.7-9; Num. 20.15-16) with a
few Deuteronomic phrases (cp. 4.34).

It is then first-fruits of the land which God has given to
his people which the Israelite is bringing, and it is to this God
alone that they can be brought.  Here is the opportunity of
thankful rejoicing before God in that family worship, including Levite and stranger which is characteristic of Deuteronomy
(cp. 12.1-12, 18; 16.11, 14).  In this book, says Buchanan
Gray,[1] first-fruits 'are the symbol of what Yahweh has given
the Israelites, or rather a representative portion of the entire
gift of Yahweh brought into his presence, that in the presence
of both the gift and the divine giver he may solemnly and
gratefully acknowledge the goodness of God.'

For the Christian this form of service makes clear that the
giver of the good gifts of the creation is the God who has
made himself known in history.  If ever we reject that historical revelation for a supposedly more direct relation to the
God of the universe as it is, we come not nearer to the true
God, but farther away from him.  The God who redeemed
Israel is the Lord of heaven and earth.

But, also, this form of service is the testimony to an accomplished redemption.  God has delivered his people from
slavery in Egypt into the freedom and prosperity of the
promised land.  The Christian thankfully acknowledges that
redemption, the deliverance from the darkness of sin into
peace and joy in Christ.  He too is asked to bring the fruits
which that redemption has made possible and offer them to
the one true God.

### 26.12-15  The Blessing of God upon the faithful Israelite

When the Israelite makes his tithe for the poor, every third
year (14.28) probably at the feast of booths (A.V. Tabernacles) (16.13-15), he is to come and confess before God that
he has done so.  What is needed for tithes to be given to the
Levite, and the stranger, the fatherless and the widow, is
'hallowed', not available for common purposes, and he has
put it away.  He has neither forgotten nor trangressed God's

[1] *Sacrifice in the Old Testament*, p. 47.

commandments. Nor has he transgressed demands of ritual purity (1) by eating the tithe when ritually unclean as a mourner for the dead, or (2) by separating it when ritually unclean (read with R.V. 'neither have I put away thereof, being unclean'); or (3) given anything of it for the dead—either by giving some of it to a mourning feast (see II Sam. 3.35; Jer. 16.7-8; Ezek. 24.17), or by offering food at the grave as if it were to be eaten by the dead (Tob. 4.17; Ecclus. 30.18). Indeed, he repeats he has done all that Yahweh his God has commanded him.

So he prays for the blessing of God to fall upon Israel's land, given by God in fulfilment of his promise. Israel's prosperity depends upon the blessing of God. It is those who are most concerned to keep the commandments of God, who have most right to pray for that blessing.

We are told in the Mishnah[2] that John Hyrcanus (High Priest 135-104 B.C.) did away with the declaration. It was probably in many cases false, since the law was not in fact being obeyed. The practice of later times is described in the Palestinian Talmud.[3] Up to verse 14 the declaration was said in a low voice: verse 15 was said in a raised voice. The explanation seems to be that the silence of those who had not tithed would be noticeable if everyone else said the verses aloud. All could join in verse 15 which is an appeal to God's goodness.

What is the relation to this passage of the Parable of the Pharisee and the Publican (Luke 17.9-14)? T. W. Manson says:[4] ' The unpleasant feature in the prayer is the self-satisfied comparison which the Pharisee makes between himself and those who do not belong to his party. It is, unhappily, very easy to slip from " There, but for the grace of God goes John Bradford " to, " God, I thank thee that I am not as the rest of men ". . . . This publican was a rotter; and he knew it. He asked for God's mercy because mercy was the only thing he dared ask for. . . . Why does the publican go down justified

[2] Ma ᶜaser Sheni, v. 10-15.
[3] Ma ᶜaser Sheni, 5, 56d 25.
[4] ' The Sayings of Jesus ' in *The Mission and Message of Jesus*, pp. 602, 604.

rather than the Pharisee? The answer is that the decisive thing is not the past record, whether good or bad, but the present attitude towards God.'

The form of service in these verses makes no unworthy comparisons and it does ask for the blessing of God. It easily lends itself to the sins of pride and hypocrisy, but it does express something real. It is better to be faithful in the performance of religious duties, especially if they make obligatory a living concern for the well-being of others, than to be unfaithful. The teaching of Jesus supplements Deuteronomy without setting it aside. No faithful obedience is a substitute for present humble waiting upon God and trust in his mercy.

# VII

## THE COVENANT OBLIGATIONS OF
## GOD AND HIS PEOPLE
### 26.16-19

The fundamental covenant for the Deuteronomist is the covenant at Horeb: all else is commentary upon it. There was an earlier covenant made with the fathers to give Israel the promised land (see 4.13; 7.12; cp. also 1.8; 6.10), but the covenant at Horeb is the decisive action of God in entering into relationship with his people. The word 'berith'—covenant—is not used here, but it is implied. Just as 'torah' (instruction, law) has widening circles of meaning, so has 'covenant', with the difference that the wider covenants are attempts to express what is implicit in the fundamental covenant.

The relationship between God and his people, acknowledged in Moab in the promulgation and acceptance of laws expanding and applying the fundamental covenant at Horeb, is one of mutual obligation. The Hebrew word translated 'avouched' means 'caused to say', which may be translated 'acknowledge', except that it seems that Yahweh has acknowledged that he is Israel's God, and that Israel has acknowledged that they are Yahweh's people (cp. 7.6). The choice is not forced upon the God of Israel, because it is his decision to be their God, out of his free grace: and nothing that Israel can do can make him withdraw his determination to be their God.

On Israel's part, both Yahweh's acknowledgement that he is their God, and that they are his people, bind them to go his way and to do his will. Israel has committed itself to HEARKEN UNTO HIS VOICE—to listen to what he says. In a world of many conflicting voices, Israel has promised to listen to God and to go his way. On that listening and obeying depends its distinctive life.

147

Yahweh is to make Israel high above all nations 'for a praise, and for a name, and for an honour (R.V. marg.), that is, to himself (cp. Jer. 13.11)'. The function of Israel is to make the name of God hallowed. S. R. Driver says: 'From its position, the condition of being a holy people to Jehovah appears to be viewed here as a privilege conferred upon Israel by God (cp. 28.9), rather than as a duty (which it is Israel's part to realize for itself (14.2, 21).' The substitution of pride in privilege for humble obedience even to death is an ever-present danger to those who are called of God.

Wheeler Robinson says: [1] 'The conception of the covenant which underlies the Book of Deuteronomy (especially seen in Deut. 26.17-18) extends the terms of the covenant made at Sinai in ethical demand along prophetic lines and, in particular, emphasizes the divine grace in the election of Israel: " Yahweh did not set His love upon you, nor choose you, because ye were more in number than any people; for ye were the fewest of all peoples: but because Yahweh loveth you " (Deut. 7.7-8).'

Adam Welch says: [2] 'Each act in which a man in Israel shows himself conscious of God's mercy to him and of God's will for him is something in which he avouches himself anew the heir of the life that has sustained all his nation's history. . . I think every Christian man knows that sense in the Holy Communion, and the power of a simple ritual in which something is done which has only been done by men who own a common faith. . . The Church, in a symbolic act of its corporate life, feels the centuries vanish in the presence of something that God has done for men, and serves itself heir to a life which is not of to-day nor of yesterday, for it has been in all the genera-tions which have done this in remembrance, and shall be in all the generations which do it to the end.'

---

[1] *Redemption and Revelation*, p. 226.
[2] *The Religion of Israel under the Kingdom*, pp. 218-19.

# PART THREE

## THE BLESSING AND THE CURSE
### 27.1-30.20

In this part of the Book of Deuteronomy a number of chapters from different hands are grouped together round the theme of the blessing and the curse, and this is fundamental to the original book (cp. 11.1-32). The ideas of blessing and curse go back to very ancient times, and were liable to be used in the interest of magic controlled by man. The whole movement of Revelation in Old Testament and New is to reverse this tendency. Ultimately the blessing of God is his grace or personal favour towards man (cp. Norman Snaith, *The Distinctive Ideas of the Old Testament*) and the curse is the absence of God's grace or, as it is called in the New Testament, the Wrath (on the meaning of the Wrath contrast C. H. Dodd, *Romans, Moffatt New Testament Commentary*, pp. 20-4, with Edwyn Bevan, *Symbolism and Belief*, chaps. ix, x).

## VIII

## THE LAW AND THE CURSES
### 27.1-26

### 27.1-13 Interruption: Making known the Law in the Promised Land

This section interrupts the natural flow of thought and language between chapters 26 and 28. Its theme is important and relevant to Deuteronomy but not here. Moses is referred to in the third person, and the section is not a literary unity.

The command to set up stones on the day Jordan is crossed, and to set them on Mount Ebal, is not necessarily a double command; the writer may have thought of Mount Ebal as being nearer to the river Jordan than it is. Whitewashed limestone might be suitable for writing in Egypt, but it is not suitable for the climate of Palestine, where only inscriptions in basalt have endured. This may be an early tradition.

For Mount Ebal the Samaritan Pentateuch reads Mount Gerizim, their sacred mountain (referred to in John 4.20). Mount Ebal was evidently once a very important sanctuary, owing to the central position of Shechem, but later it was neglected. History is seldom as tidy as later theology would like to make it.

**5-7** belong to a different source from the rest, and the building of an altar at Mount Ebal is not to be reconciled with the law of the altar (chap. 12), unless, indeed, the original reference to the place where Yahweh would choose to set his name was not in Jerusalem, but a shrine of the Northern Kingdom. The injunction is alien to the early law in Ex. 20.24-25. Unhewn stones were supposed to be more sacred than ones which have had to be cut: the worship is characteristic of Deuteronomy. How much was implied in the phrase ' all the words of this law ' we do not know.

**9-10** which suggest that the proclamation of the law in the Promised Land is a further covenantal experience, and repeat the theme of Deuteronomy that to be the people of God implies obedience to him, are in keeping with chapter 26, but do not add anything to what is said there.

**11-13** emphasize the importance of the choice between blessing and curse by reference to a ceremony to be performed on Mount Gerizim and Mount Ebal. Note also that the story of the Patriarchs brings Abraham and Jacob straight to Shechem (Gen. 12.6; 33.18). The contrast of the two mountains is to be used to symbolize the blessing and the curse. These verses come from an early source, when Simeon and Levi are still existent tribes. The whole of vv. 1-13 are referred to in Josh. 8.30-35, which presupposes the written book, and asserts that this ceremony was actually carried out.

### 27.14-26  Insertion of different subject-matter.  Unconditional Curses on individual wrongdoing

This section does not follow on from the preceding, because there Levi is a tribe; here Levites are a religious order.  By comparison, the curses to be found in chapter 28 are national and conditional upon disobedience, whereas the curses here are unconditional and fall upon the individual. The passage is probably part of an old liturgical document. The curses are mostly directed against secret sins which would not be brought before a human tribunal. The curse, in ancient thought, had a magical power to vindicate itself, and the individual who believed that, especially if he had helped to pronounce the curse, would be smitten in his own conscience by it. The word 'Amen', signifying the assent of the people, is literally an adjective meaning 'firm', then used adverbially it means 'verily' (I Kings 1.36; Jer. 11.5) and then it becomes a liturgical response, as here (Num. 5.22, Neh. 8.6, Ps. 106.48).

The curses are not specially related to the concern of Deuteronomy, though they all have some sort of parallel in some part of the laws of the Pentateuch. S. R. Driver says: 'The parallels agree in substance, but the resemblance is seldom verbal: hence the imprecations will hardly have been taken directly from the corresponding prohibitions.'

**15.** The cursing of secret worshipping of images probably did not belong to the original list. It was added after the denunciation of public worship of images had been accepted (cp. 4.16, 5.8, 9.12).

**16.** Setting light by father or mother breaks the fifth commandment (v. 16). v. 17 corresponds to the law against removing boundary stones in 19.14. v. 18 The nearest equivalent is Lev. 19.14, 'thou shalt not put a stumbling-block before the blind.' v. 19 corresponds to the law of 24.17 against wresting the judgment of the stranger, the fatherless and the widow. v. 20 corresponds to the law of 22.30 against a man's marrying his stepmother. v. 21 against bestiality is paralleled in Ex. 22.19, Lev. 18.13, 20.15-16. v. 22 against marriage with a half-sister is paralleled in Lev. 18.9, 20.17; it was allowed in earlier times in Israel (Gen. 20.12, II Sam. 13.12-13). v. 23 against marriage with a mother-in-law is paralleled in Lev. 18.17, 20.14. v. 24 against smiting our neighbour secretly is roughly paralleled by the ninth commandment against false witness (v. 20) and more nearly by 19.11. v. 25 against taking

payment to slay an innocent person has only broad warrant
in the laws against tribes (16.19, Ex. 23.18).   v. 26 is not a
specific requirement but a general curse against not keeping
the Deuteronomic law.   We may compare King Josiah's 'covenant to perform all the words that were written in the book' (II
Kings 23.3, 24).

**26** is one of the series of quotations used by St. Paul in his
argument in Gal. 3.1-14, to show that Christ has removed the
curse of the law.   We have already met this in 21.22-23.   Here
we may admit that there is a curse of the law against those who
do not fulfil its requirements, and that Paul is right in principle
in insisting that our ultimate reliance must not be upon our
obedience, but upon the mercy of God.   What we must say
also is that this truth is the heart of the Old Covenant as well
as of the New, and that Paul's basis of argument is not in
conflict with the Old Covenant, but rooted in an incomparably
richer manifestation of the mercy of God.

Two things must be said about the levitical curses.   They
are an expression of those things which are condemned by the
conscience of the community.   They may or may not bring a
man into conflict with the legal system, but they are things
which the community as a whole reprobates.   The higher the
standard set here, provided that the community lives by it
without strain, the better.   Some things which have been repro-
bated down the centuries we may hope will continue to be
regarded with horror, but we have experienced some retro-
gression in the present century, and we cannot take for granted
that we shall preserve undiminished our moral tradition, still less
improve upon it.   What is important is that our community shall
repudiate all practices which are a degradation of human life.

In addition, these curses claim the assent of the individual
conscience to the repudiation of evil.   It is what people do in
secret which is the testing place of their character.   What we do
in secret from our fellows is not hidden from God—and hidden
sin, in the end, brings its fruit to light.   The opposite is also
true.   In the secret place, the heart is renewed in faith and
love from God.   'Pray to thy Father which is in secret, and
thy Father which seeth in secret shall recompense thee.'

# THE BLESSINGS OF OBEYING GOD AND THE CURSES OF DISOBEYING HIM

## 28.1-68

The blessing of God is not unconditional. He awaits man's response.

The Book of Deuteronomy is in harmony with the other laws in the Pentateuch in ending with a statement of the alternative. The peroration to the earlier laws given in Ex. 23.20-33 contains only a hint of the possibilities of disobedience, and expounds the positive results of obedience. The peroration to the later laws given in Lev. 26.3-45, which has affinities with Ezekiel as this chapter has with Jeremiah, develops the sombre side of the alternative, though it ends with the possibility of restoration. This chapter, like that of Leviticus, is one of sustained eloquence, bringing home, in a moving way, the darker possibilities of life.

It is likely that the chapter, in its present form, contains additions to the original—the curses have been added to by later writers. It is a grim comment upon human history that men should feel that the curses of life have not been made sufficiently explicit: no one seems to have had the same urgency to declare that the blessings of life have been unduly minimized. It is, however, clear that some severe curses were part of the Book of the Law discovered in the Temple in 621 (see II Kings 22.13, Jer. 11.3).

Schalom Ben-Chorim in an open letter to Max Brod says:[1] 'You perhaps remember asking me late one evening in Tel-Aviv what passage in scripture made me feel the word of God breaking into human speech. And without hesitation I answered you; the Tochacha, the 28th chapter of curses in Deuteronomy. Here the destiny of Israel, which is without analogy, is foretold down to the present day.' And he adds: 'How strangely

[1] In *Comfort ye, Comfort ye, My People*: Jerusalem, 1943, pp. 16-18.

interdependent are judgment and grace.' Surely Christians
too can find, in this unfolding of the tragic possibilities of life,
the witness of the Spirit.

### 28.1-14  The blessings of obeying God: Israel shall be strong, happy and successful

If Israel will be obedient, God will set the nation on high, and
will make prosperity overtake it in every part of the national
life.  Israel's enemies will be smitten, and God will bless Israel
in the Promised Land.  Israel will be God's people, and the
name of Yahweh will be called over them (A.V. 'Thou art
called by the name of the Lord') to show his ownership (cp. II
Sam. 12.28 R.V. marg., I Kings 7.43).  Israel will be fertile
and prosperous beyond other nations, and have their respect.

In v. 12 for A.V. 'treasure' read 'treasury' with R.V.
marg.

The blessings obviously refer to the condition of life during
the Kingdom because the blessings are meant to maintain and
increase agricultural security.  Israel is in possession of its
own land and able to direct its own life and maintain its own
institutions.  This has come through the God of Israel, and
only through continued obedience to him could Israel be
strong and free.

Matthew Henry says: 'Though temporal blessings do not
take up so much room in the promises of the New Testament
as they do in the Old, yet it is enough that our Lord Jesus
has given us his word (and sure we may take his word) that if
we seek first the kingdom of God, and the righteousness
thereof, all other things shall be added to us, as far as infinite
wisdom sees good, and who can desire it further?   (Matt. 6.33).'

The most important blessing is that God SHALL ESTABLISH
THEE A PEOPLE UNTO HIMSELF (v. 9).  The understanding of
what this implies does not go very deep here, but it is capable
of great enrichment. Whatever the trials of the church militant,
God's blessing of his people to make them a holy people to
himself cannot fail.  For the fulness of that blessing we must
wait till the consummation of all things.

**28.15-68   The curses of disobeying God**

> 15-26 Israel shall be weak and unhappy and un-
>         successful
> 27-37 life shall be one continual frustration even
>         leading to exile
> 38-46 disobedience will bring failure and subsequent
>         inferiority in Israel's own land
> 47-57 a relentless enemy will bring upon Israel the
>         last desperate horrors of a siege
> 58-68 disobedient Israel will be plagued, scattered,
>         in constant anxiety, and brought back captive
>         but unsaleable to Egypt

**15-26.** These verses form a more or less exact parallel to
the verses of the blessings; where prosperity had been promised, there will be adversity. The special element in these
curses is the plagues which shall afflict Israel. In v. 22 read
with R.V. marg. 'with drought' instead of A.V. WITH THE
SWORD. There are seven plagues and they will pursue Israel
just as the enemy of v. 25 will pursue in seven directions. v. 23
THY HEAVEN THAT IS OVER THEE SHALL BE BRASS, AND THE
EARTH THAT IS UNDER THEE SHALL BE IRON is a proverbial
description of the state of drought. On v. 24 George Adam
Smith comments : ' The Sirocco, as the present writer has more
than once encountered it in Judaea, brings up a fog of dust as
dense and fine as a sea-mist, but very destructive.' v. 25 for
A.V. REMOVED INTO read ' a horror unto ', that is, an awe-
inspiring spectacle. The expression is found in Jer. 15.4,
25.9, 29.18, 34.17. v. 26. The theme of carcases being eaten
by birds and beasts is also found in Jer. 7.33, 16.4, 19.7,
34.20.

**27-37** express an experience of inescapable frustration. It
is probably an interpretation of what it means to be an enemy-
occupied country. Israel is not its own master, and suffers
accordingly. In our day we have known by personal experience
what it is for nations to be afflicted with MADNESS AND BLIND-
NESS AND ASTONISHMENT OF HEART and to GROPE IN DARKNESS
AT NOONDAY; and we know that it can be real for people, that
their eyes look for their loved ones and fail with longing for

them all the day. Adam Welch says:[2] 'In language of that
intensity and power we are conscious of listening to a proud
nation writhing under the sense of its helplessness.'

The diseases in v. 27 may be translated 'boils, and ulcers,
scurvy and itch', but the general reader may be content with
'the disease of Egypt and other sorts of skin diseases' of the
Bible in Basic English. v. 35, which mentions more diseases,
seems to be an intrusion where it is. (cp. the diseases of Job
2.7-8, 7.3-6, 19.17-20, 30.17.)

In vv. 36-37 we have a prophecy of exile for the nation with
its king which will cause Israel to be an object of scorn and
derision. The first Jewish kings to be deported were, so far as
we know, Jehoahaz in 608 B.C. to Egypt (II Kings 23.34) and
Jehoiachim in 597 B.C. to Babylon (II Kings 24.8-16); but there
was a large deportation of the people of Judah in 701. These
verses do not imply any experience of exile. Dr. Welch says:[3]
'However men in Israel may have made the worship of the
heathen gods the inevitable result of the exile before the event
happened, the actual experience of exile was sufficient to confute
their fears. It is an interesting illustration of the way in which
experience often refutes theory to notice that, at the very time
when men in Jerusalem were counting the exiles "rotten figs
because they were getting cut off from the temple and all the
means of grace", those exiles were getting into trouble in
Babylonia because of their determined loyalty to their own
religion. For "fears may be liars".'

**38-46** presuppose the same conditions as vv. 15-26. Here
the Promised Land goes bad on Israel. Its characteristic
products, corn, wine, and oil (see 7.13 and cp. Hos. 2) shall not
be available for the inhabitants (v. 41 which is similar to v. 32
and treats of sons and daughters going into captivity is an
intrusion here). The stranger, the domiciled foreigner, whom
Deuteronomy has so often commended to Israel's consideration, because he does not depend on the land, will profit through
trade at Israel's expense and dominate Israel in its own land.

**45-46** form a natural close to a series of curses, and may be

[2] *Deuteronomy: the Framework to the Code*, p. 135.
[3] *op. cit.*, p. 134n.

the original stopping-place. The curses will be a sign of
God's judgment and a wonder, arousing men's horror at Israel's
fate.

**47-57.** Since Israel has not served God with gladness, it
must serve a fierce enemy, starving, naked, and destitute. In
language akin to that of Jeremiah (with v. 49 cp. Jer. 5.15;
with v. 51 cp. Jer. 5.17; with v. 53 cp. Jer. 19.9) it describes
the impact of a cruel enemy.    (In v. 49 for A.V. AS SWIFT AS THE
EAGLE FLIETH read 'as the vulture swoopeth'.)  Finally it
describes the last extremities in eating human flesh to which a
siege drives the inhabitants.  For such practices see II Kings
6.24-30, Lam. 4.10.  (In v. 56 for WHICH WOULD NOT ADVEN-
TURE read 'who had never ventured' to set the sole of her foot
upon the ground, i.e. because she had always been carried.
In v. 57 for YOUNG ONE read with R.V. marg. 'after-birth'.)
This passage was written from personal experience.  There
is a note of horror and pain in it which the reader cannot fail
to note.  But the internal evidence gives us no clue to the date
of the siege.  It may be the siege of Jerusalem in 588-6; it
might just as easily be the siege of Samaria by Sargon in 722.

Adam Welch says:[4] 'What is especially noteworthy is that
the men were prepared to acknowledge that what they suffered
was not unmerited; the estate to which they have been reduced
was the proof of the righteous anger of their God.  In that
very acknowledgement there is an indomitable note.'  This,
however, is only true when in addition to the acknowledgement
of the judgment of God, there is a determination to change
those same conditions for the better in the name of God.

**58-68.** The author of this section makes clear the purpose
of the law—to 'fear this glorious and fearful name, Yahweh
thy God'.  (On the glory of God's name see Neh. 9.5, Ps. 70.11,
19, I Chron. 29.13, Isa. 63.12, Ex. 33.18-19: on fearing the
Name see Mal. 4.2, Isa. 59.19.)  The law is referred to in two
places as written, vv. 58 and 61 (as also in 29.20, 21, 27;
30.10), but this contradicts the general presupposition that
Moses spoke the laws which finds explicit expression in 31.1-9.

The section threatens to bring on Israel every kind of sick-

[4] *Deuteronomy: the Framework to the Code*, p. 137.

ness, especially the diseases of Egypt (cp. 7.15). This will
reduce Israel to the few from which they began (4.27) revers-
ing God's redemptive act (26.5).

**63** is a terrible saying. As God rejoiced to do Israel good,
so he rejoiced to destroy them. This is in direct conflict with
prophetic teaching, especially the teaching of Hosea (see Hos.
11.8-9), and it is not characteristic of the teaching of Deuteronomy. God has no joy in the destruction of his people, even
when they disobey.

**64-67.** Israel will be scattered in exile, and live there in
perpetual anxiety. This is a vivid statement. Life hangs by a
single thread. The present is unendurable because of the
danger that threatens on every side, the future is even worse,
because the imagination dwells on possible horrors.

**68.** The worst may happen. Israel may even be carried in
slave-ships back to Egypt, that house of bondage, escape from
which constituted the distinctive element in Israel's history.
God had said there must be no going back to Egypt (cp.
17.16). But it has happened. And even the Egyptians are so
appalled at the penalty for disobeying God that no one will
buy them as slaves.

The best epitome of this long series of parallel curses in
vv. 15-68 is the word of St. Paul (Rom. 1.18), ' The wrath of
God is revealed from heaven against all ungodliness and unrighteousness of men.' It is a grievous thing to disobey the
will of the living God. The original Book of Deuteronomy
ends with the most solemn warning against disobedience.

What meaning has this chapter for us to-day? Here are
real experiences—the happiness and affliction of mankind in
our earthly pilgrimage. The theory of how they are related
to God is too narrow for us to live by. We have learnt that
chance, goodwill or ill will of others, and capacity or incapacity
on our own part play a larger and more immediate part in
determining success or failure, prosperity or adversity, than is
here recognized. Also from the experience of the Exile, from
the experience of an individual sufferer like Job, above all,
from the fact of the Crucifixion, we have learnt that we cannot
always ascribe suffering to the wrath of God, and that the

voluntary acceptance of suffering and death may be necessary to fulfil the call of God.

Where the chapter has its justification is that in the end its presupposition that to obey God brings blessing, to disobey him brings curse is absolutely right. Even here, ' upon this bank and shoal of time ' (Macbeth i.7) this is made plain from time to time for men to see; and though it needs eternity for its full vindication, it is the only true basis for our present living.

Again, we need the help and blessing of God when the blessings and curses of life come upon us. The blessings of life, if not handled aright, may sap our moral fibre and frustrate our purposes more than any obvious curse would do, and the curses of life, if used aright, may lose quite a large part of their sting, and may even yield positive blessing. With God's help both the blessings and the curses of life may lead us nearer to our true life which is ' hid with Christ in God '.

Moreover, we must not blink the fact that there is a blessing and a curse of God. The blessing of God is to know him, to have the character and outlook that belongs to that knowledge, and to have the joy that springs from trusting in God. The curse of God is to be frustrated in our evil purposes and to be without the strengthening of God's presence. Here we must choose and our life be determined by our choice.

We must take heed of the word of St. Paul in Gal. 3.13, ' Christ has redeemed us from the curse of the law, being made a curse for us.' Christ's acceptance of judicial condemnation for the sake of his mission to bring all men to God, opens the way by which we may be delivered from the condemnation of God into that eternal life which he rejoices to give us.

# X

## THE THIRD SPEECH OF MOSES
### 29.1-30.20

**29.1-29 Israel must live by its revelation: apostasy will bring disaster**

**1** is an editorial note which stands at the end of chapter 28 in the Hebrew Bible, making a conclusion to the covenant in Moab which elucidates the meaning of the fundamental covenant in Horeb.

**2-29** are by a later writer who is dependent on the earlier part of the book which he knows is in written form (vv. 20, 21, 27) and who knows that Israel is at present (v. 28) in exile.

    **2-9**    Now only is the meaning of God's revelation plain

    **10-15**    The Covenant of God is with all Israelites wherever they are

    **16-17**    You know the dangers

    **18-21**    The curses will fall upon the individual unbeliever

    **22-28**    The promised land will be desolate if the covenant is forsaken

    **29**    The future belongs to God: Israel lives by the revelation made to it

**2-9.** Israel has seen the mighty acts of God in delivering them from the power of Pharaoh (cp. 4.34), but it is only now that the meaning of the covenant is made plain. It is Biblical teaching that not only the act of God but the understanding of that act, not only revelation, but response, is of God. 'The light of the knowledge of the glory of God in the face of Jesus Christ' must also 'shine in our hears' (II Cor. 4.6). The comment on Peter's confession of Jesus as the Christ is 'Flesh and blood hath not revealed it unto thee, but my Father which is in heaven' (Matt. 16.17). The fact

160

that it is only now that Israel understands may be because they are 'slow of heart to perceive' (Luke 24.25) . . . God's redemption: it is not intended to belittle the activity of the human mind in perceiving God's truth. It is one thing for something mighty to have happened. It is another thing to grasp its implications. It is urgent for us to wake up and understand what God has done and is doing.

**5** is a contracted repetition of 8.2-4. The extravagance of the symbolism of God's complete care of Israel is even clearer. If we understand, with Matthew Henry, that 'those very shoes which by the appointment of God they put on in Egypt . . . never wore out but served them to Canaan', it becomes ridiculous.

The purpose of this complete dependence upon God's care is that Israel should know that he is God. (The phrase is not characteristic of Deuteronomy: it is one which occurs in Ezekiel more than fifty times.) This is the meaning of the story of Israel, that knowledge of God which involves utter commitment to living in him. The Fourth Gospel speaks of the fulfilment of this knowledge in Christ, which is set against the ignorance of Jew and Gentile alike. 'This is life eternal, that they might know thee the only true God, and Jesus Christ whom thou hast sent' (John 17.3).

The story of Sihon and Og and their land has been told in 2.32-37, 3.1-7, 12-17. In the past the wisdom and success that has been in Israel has come from God. It will be so also in the future if Israel abides faithful to God's covenant.

Israel has presented itself before God to accept the covenant that he is making with them. In v. 10 for A.V. THE CAPTAINS OF YOUR TRIBES read 'your heads, your judges'. The word 'camp' suggests the wilderness, but the mention of 'the stranger' implies the settled land. The children of the covenant are affected by its blessing and curse before they come to conscious decision. Even those with the humblest menial occupations are not excluded. The meaning of the covenant has been given in 26.17-18. The covenant is not only with those members of Israel present, but with the members of other peoples who acknowledge Israel's

L

religious loyalty, and with Israelites dispersed in other lands.
The Israelite who has been taken into exile is not outside the
reach either of the blessing or the obligations of the covenant.
Under all circumstances faith in God is our first hope and
our first duty.

**16-17** sound remote from the difficult struggle of Israel's
faith: they rest upon the victory won. For A.V. ABOMINA-
TIONS read 'detestable things '. By the side of the living God,
the acknowledgement of idols, here referred to with a con-
temptuous word, is unspeakable degradation.

**18-21.** The individual unbeliever will not escape the curses
that follow disobedience, he will be detected and his name
blotted out. May there not be a man or a woman, a family
or a tribe turned away from the true God to serve the gods
of other nations—the ever-present idolatries of the human
heart! May there not be among you a root that beareth gall
and wormwood—poison and bitter sorrow. When such a
man hears the words of this oath (not curse, A.V.) that God
will be Israel's God and will bless her continually, he will
flatter himself saying, 'I will be all right and will share in
the blessing.' Here the result of the idolator's self-con-
gratulation is expressed as if it was his purpose. He thinks
he will be all right, though he is in fact stubbornly persisting
in going his own way which he knows is against the will of
God (for A.V. 'IMAGINATION' read 'stubbornness', see Jer.
3.17, 7.24, 9.13, 11.8, 13.10, 16.12, 18.12, 23.17).

The end of that would be that good and bad would be
swept away together and all Israel would be destroyed because of individual faithlessness and selfishness (for A.V.
TO ADD DRUNKENNESS TO THIRST read 'to carry away the
watered with the parched '). In Hebrews 12.15 the phrase
'any root of bitterness' is borrowed from the Septuagint
version of v. 18. Here the trouble is self-indulgence not
idolatry, but in both cases the sanctification of the whole
must not be put in jeopardy by the poisonous influence of
one. Here, in cumulative phrases, the utter blotting out of
the man from Israel by the wrath of God is proclaimed. All
the curses of the previous chapter will fasten on to him. It

is worth noting that if these phrases are read in the context
of eternity, they are more appalling than in the original. So
far as this life is concerned the blotting out of men is a
reality, and we have to reckon with the possibility. Where
God is concerned we must insist that beyond judgment (however deep and serious that is) there is always mercy (cp. John
3.17).

**22-28.** What will the generation of Israelites to come, and
the traveller coming from distant parts say when they see
the Promised Land plainly afflicted of God? The land will
be utterly desolate and covered with sulphur and salt and lava.
It will be like the cities of the Plain, Sodom and Gomorrah
(whose destruction is told in Gen. 19.24-29. cp. Matt. 10.15,
Luke 10.12); and Admah and Zeboim (mentioned in what
George Adam Smith calls[1] ' the greatest passage in Hosea—
deepest if not highest—of his book—the breaking forth of
that exhaustless mercy of the Most High which no sin of man
can bar back nor wear out '. Hos. 11.8-9 ' How shall I make
thee as Admah? How shall I set thee as Zeboim? ' cp. Gen.
14.2). The imagery is taken from the character of the region
about the Dead Sea.[2] Ezek. (47.1-12) saw a river flowing from
the Temple to give new life to the desolate land.

Why has God done this to the Promised Land? Because
Israel has forsaken God's covenant and worshipped other gods.
So the wrath of God was kindled against the land and Israel
has been cast into exile. It is important to realize that this
conviction is only partially true. God is very patient, and the
sin of man is not the only thing that brings about his own
downfall. Just as we do well to find out the material situation
and physical condition of men before giving moral judgments
on their actions, so we do well to survey other possible factors
in an historical situation besides disobedience to God. But if
the writer of this passage was liable to over-estimate this, we
are liable to under-estimate it. The rejection of the moral
claim of God is a real factor in human history and its conse-

---

[1] *The Book of the Twelve Prophets*, vol. 1, p. 297.
[2] See George Adam Smith, *Historical Geography of the Holy Land*,
pp. 257-8.

quences are deeply serious. We must reckon with the element
of unfaithfulness in ourselves and in our people.

**29** states a principle which Judaism and Christianity have
in common. What the future will bring upon us we cannot
tell. There are many unsolved mysteries which we cannot
fathom. We believe that they are all under the control of
God and that we may safely leave them to him. What we do
know is the positive way of faith and life which has been
revealed to us. Only by faithful and glad acceptance of the
meaning of life as God has given it to us, can we hope to
harvest the opportunities of the present. Whatever our perplexities and uncertainties, we know our covenant relation to
God—for this writer it was the Deuteronomic covenant, for
us it is Christ the way, the truth, and the life. It does not
matter if we are ignorant of times and seasons, if the Holy
Spirit is come upon us (Acts 1.7-8).

**30.1-20   The choice of life or death is always before us**
             1-10 repentance will bring restoration
             11-14 the demand of God is for something within
                   our reach
             15-20 the choice before us is between life and death
When all the blessing and the curse spoken of in chap. 28 have
happened, the blessing because God has been with his people,
the curse because that is the immediately present fact, and
Israel remembers them in exile and returns to a new living
faith in God, then Israel can rely upon the compassion of
God. What distinguishes this faith and its greater expression
in the New Testament from all other outlooks on life is that it
sets the divine compassion at the heart of life. The compassion
of God is not soft and empty, it is not the plaything of man's
self-indulgence; it expresses the fact that in man's deepest need
he has to do with a God who cares and who will renew the
springs of life of his people.

In v. 3 for A.V. TURN THY CAPTIVITY read 'change thy
fortune'. Even the uttermost (A.V. OUTMOST) parts of the
heaven are not too far away for God to gather his people. v. 4
with this thought has been used in the composition of Nehe-

miah's prayer (Neh. 1.9), and it is used in the thought of the
gathering of God's elect at the coming of the Son of Man
(Mark 13.27, Matt. 24.31). And God will bring them again
into the Promised Land and they will be even more prosperous
than before.

6. Above all, God will give them a circumcised heart, a
heart from which all false pride has been taken away and they
will be able to love their God with all their heart and with all
their soul. We may compare this with Ezek. 11.19-20. 'And
I will give them one heart, and I will put a new spirit within
you; and I will take the stony heart out of their flesh: that
they may walk in my statutes, and keep mine ordinances and
do them: and they shall be my people, and I will be as their
God' (cp. also Ezek. 36.26-27, and Jer. 24.7 and 31.31-34).

What the writer is saying is that God will give them not only
his own faithful love, but also the actual presence of an utterly
faithful answering love in their own hearts. This is the longing
of every man of faith. But it is only imperfectly fulfilled here
below; it will not be completely fulfilled till that day when
because we see him as he is, we shall be like him (I John 3.2).
What is important is that we must not oppose the Covenant at Horeb and at Moab and the New Covenant as material
outward covenants to the circumcised heart, Jeremiah's New
Covenant, and Ezekiel's heart of flesh. The promise of the
circumcised heart is the promise that the revealed covenant
which is the ground of our faith and trust, shall be filled with
all the love and devotion of which God can make us capable.

In v. 7 we are brought back to Deuteronomy's limited vision
—the curses which God removes from Israel shall be put on
Israel's enemies. He has not seen that they also are God's
children. In v. 8 THOU SHALT RETURN AND OBEY THE VOICE OF
THE LORD 'return' probably means 'return in mind and heart
to God' (cp. Isa. 10.27, 19.22, Jer. 3.1-7). In v. 9 Israel will have
the blessings promised in 28.1-14 and God will rejoice over
Israel for good (cp. 28.63a). Israel must keep the laws written
in Deuteronomy, and turn to its God with heart and soul.

11-14 may not have been originally linked with the fore-
going, but they have added point if we think they are, and

that they were addressed to Israel in exile. Were they outside
the realm where Yahweh ruled as God? Was there any possibility of their doing his will in exile? Yes. The fundamental
requirement of the covenant was to love God with heart and
soul, and that was not a matter so exalted or distant that they
could not attempt it: it was on their lips whenever they
wrestled with the problem of their fate, and it was the un-
spoken longing of their hearts. And even the detailed and
elaborated covenant was in their minds because it had been
diligently taught from father to son, and even in exile they
could exhibit the distinctive practices of the people of God.
(On the clearness, straightforwardness and effectiveness of the
word of God cp. Isa. 45.19.)

This passage is freely adapted by St. Paul in Rom. 10.6-8 to
help his argument that Christ has put an end to law so that
righteousness should be available to every believer. He is
really contrasting Leviticus 18.5, ' Ye shall therefore keep my
statutes and my judgments: which if a man do he shall live in
them ', with this Deuteronomic passage. Of course, Deuteronomy is as much concerned with law as is Leviticus, but there
is a contrast within the Old Testament itself between obedience,
as the ultimate word, and the love of God which goes out
beyond his people's obedience. In that contrast Paul summons
to his aid the Deuteronomic passage on the nearness to the
human heart of response to God. The Biblical teaching is a
Gospel of grace. This is right, but Paul is not right in trying
to give the Deuteronomic passage a hidden meaning which is
a direct prophecy of Christ. The argument can only be one
of analogy. As God in the Deuteronomic covenant is very
near to his people, so God in Christ, the living Lord of his
people, is always near.

In vv. 15-20 the message of the Book of Deuteronomy is
summarized for us. God summons us to choose for or against
him. The issue is one of life or death. This indeed is the
message of the whole Bible. In both Testaments God offers
the choice of life or death. We do right in noticing that the
New Testament understanding of the possibilities of life and
the possibilities of death are much profounder than that of

Deuteronomy. Here as in Jer. 21.8 life and death may be literal survival and destruction, as good and evil mean prosperity and its opposite. It seems a far cry to Col. 3.3, ' Your life is hid with Christ in God,' or to Gal. 2.20, ' The life which I now live in the flesh I live by the faith of the Son of God, who loved me and gave himself for me.'

But the contrast can be over-stressed. From the divine side God has offered to his people the choice of life and death all down their long history, and, however men have interpreted it, it is a choice between sharing in his life or being excluded from his presence. In the end God has nothing else to offer. The New Covenant in Christ is not a new offer on God's part. The gift which has only been partially conveyed and partially received is now available in all its completeness.

The choice of life and death. That is the seriousness, the urgency, and the hope of our human living. If we take seriously God's invitation to share in his own life, we must also take seriously the possibility of perishing. This will not merely mean the death of the body, but the emptying of our very existence as human beings. If beyond this, there is the prospect of complete salvation, of God being all in all, we must be clear that this is a mystery, and that it lies beyond the consequences of our having chosen the way of death.

In v. 18 for DENOUNCE read ' announce '. In v. 19 heaven and earth are witnesses to the choice to which Israel is called. If this passage was written for exiles, it derives added point by its insistence, that wherever we are and whatever our condition, the choice is still open to us. It is never too late to choose for God. The chapter ends on the positive note. The purpose of God setting this choice before his people is that Israel should learn to love the Lord her God, to obey his voice and to cleave to him—that his people may dwell in the land of promise.

# APPENDIX

## POETRY OF THE COVENANT AND THE
## DEATH OF MOSES
### 31.1-34.12

These last four chapters have only a limited connection with
Deuteronomy proper. Their basis is the older tradition of
Israel, supplemented by Deuteronomic elements, and with
some influence of the later tradition. Here Deuteronomy is
brought into touch with the general narrative of the Pentateuch—we should have expected an account of the death of
Moses after Num. 27.12-23, but it has been delayed till now—
and prepares the way for the book of Joshua.

**31.1-30  Moses and Joshua, the law-book handed over, and
Israel's faithlessness predicted**

     1-8 Moses appoints Joshua leader of Israel
     9-13 The law to be read every seven years
   14-15, 23 God's commission to Joshua
    16-22 The Song a witness against Israel
    24-26 The disposal of the law book
     2-29 The rebellion of Israel
     30 Introduction to Moses' Song

**1-8.** Moses, growing old, appoints Joshua leader in his
place, and reminds Israel and Joshua that God, who has been
with them up to now, will go before them and ensure their
success. v. 1 looks back to what has gone before, though we
cannot tell to what words of Moses it refers. Perhaps we should
read with the Septuagint that Moses 'finished speaking'. v. 2.
Moses is said to be one hundred and twenty years old (cp
34.7). This is a round figure, meaning that his life spanned
three generations. He is growing old and needs to hand over
to Joshua. The later account (34.7) represents him as continuing in full vigour and vitality till the last moment.

God has already told Moses that he will not go over Jordan (3.27, cp. 1.37, 4.21-22). God will go over before his people and win the victory for them (cp. 3.22) and Joshua will lead Israel into the land as God has said (3.28). The victories over Sihon (2.32-37) and Og (3.1-7) are examples of what will happen to the peoples opposing them, and Israel can practise upon these peoples the commandment of extermination to preserve the purity of their own faith laid down in 7.1-5.

Israel is to be full of courage, because the God of Israel will never fail them (i.e. allow them to fall) nor forsake them (cp. 4.31). This is the abiding message of the faith of Israel which survives all limitations and distortions—the abiding faithfulness and nearness of the Eternal God. Man's lack of trust here produces inevitably lack of responsible trust in his own possibilities of goodness.

Moses charges Joshua not to fail either God or Israel. He, as the leader of Israel, must be of good courage and trust in God. His function in the story of Israel is to cause Israel to inherit the land. Moses had led his people to the Promised Land; but it was Joshua, under whose leadership they actually would enter it (cp. 3.21-22, 28).

**9-13** probably give the original Deuteronomic provision for the communication and observance of the laws and exhortations laid down in this book. It was given into the hands of those recognized by Deuteronomy to be priests (the sons of Levi; cp. 18.1) and to the elders—the civil leaders of Israel (cp. 1.15). It was to be read every seven years in the year of release (15.1-6) and to be read at the feast of booths (A.V. TABERNACLES 15.13-15).

The reading, and then the interpretation and application of the written word, have been a characteristic of, and a source of immense vitality to Judaism and Christianity. The written word is not meant to quench the Spirit but to open the way for his having free course and being glorified. If the time ever comes when the written word no longer illuminates God's present dealings with us, then it is dead and nothing can bring it to life.

All—men, women and children, and the stranger—must be

gathered together to hear, and learn, and reverence God, and
do what the law requires. Especially must a deep reverence
for God and his law be communicated to Israel's children:
this is one of the abiding concerns of the Deuteronomist (see
4.9, 6.7.20-25, 11.19, 32.46).

We, in our day, cannot afford to be less concerned to transmit to our children faith in the living God and in the distinctive
life he gives and requires. But we can only do so if we are
convinced of the urgent necessity and glad reality of that faith
for the adult life we ourselves are living.

In vv. 14, 15, 23 we have the insertion of an earlier tradition
according to which God had directly commissioned Joshua to
take over the leadership of Israel from Moses. Moses and
Joshua have to present themselves at the Tent of Meeting
(A.V. the tabernacle of the congregation) and God meets with
them, and (v. 23) charges Joshua to be brave, to bring Israel
into the Promised Land, relying on his presence with him.

THE TENT OF MEETING is not otherwise met with in Deuteronomy, but is to be found in the earlier tradition (cp. Ex. 33.7-
11) and very frequently, and with great elaboration, in the
later tradition (see, for example, Ex. 26-27). The later explanation of the purpose of the tent of meeting (cp. Ex. 29.42) is
that it is where God met Moses to speak with him, so that the
tent of meeting is practically equivalent to 'the tent of
revelation'.

There are a number of traditions associating 'cloud' with
God's presence. According to one early tradition God went
before Israel in a pillar of cloud by day, and in a pillar of fire
by night (Ex. 13.21, Num. 14.14). According to another early
tradition, as here, the cloud came down and stood at the door
of the tent of meeting (Ex. 33.7-11, Num. 11.25, 12.5.10).
Both early traditions associate cloud with the revelation at
Horeb-Sinai (Ex. 34.5, 19.9.16).

In Deuteronomy elsewhere there is only a brief reference to
the cloud by day, and the fire by night (1.33) and mention of
the cloud upon Horeb (4.11, 5.22). In the later tradition the
cloud covered the glory of God on Mount Sinai (Ex. 24.16-18);
it did not come into the camp till the Tent of Meeting was

finished, when it covered the glory of God in it, and at night
had a fiery appearance (Ex. 40.34-38); the rising of the cloud
above the tent gave the signal for moving camp (Num. 9.15-23).

This early tradition of God's commission to Joshua is different from that met with elsewhere in Deuteronomy (1.38, 3.21-
22.28 and vv. 7-8 of this chapter) according to which the commission to Joshua came through Moses. The later tradition
(Num. 27.15-23) is different again in that Moses only transmits
a part of his authority to Joshua who is made subordinate to
Eleazer the priest through whom God's will is to be revealed.
It ought to be noted that there is no real opposition between
being commissioned by God and being commissioned through
other men though, as a matter of history, they have not always
coincided (cp. Gal. 1.11-24).

In vv. 16-22 God tells Moses that after his death Israel will
forsake the covenant and that he will bring evil upon them.
They will to some extent acknowledge that the cause of their
distress is that God's presence has left them, but they will not
really turn to him in penitence. So God commands Moses to
write the Song of the next chapter to be a witness against
Israel.

This misunderstands the purpose of the Song, which is one
of comfort, and not denunciation; and does violence to the
situation of the farewell between Moses and his people, however much the intention was to glorify Moses' fame as a
prophet. The passage comes from one writing from the safe
vantage point of centuries later, who neglects the struggle and
achievement of Israel's story, and sees only the failure by the
highest standards of a later time.

Of course, there is truth in it. The story of man's relation
with God must be one of struggle to keep faithful to that one
central loyalty—the great commandment: thou shalt love the
Lord thy God. The phrase GO A-WHORING may have originated
in a reference to sexual excesses at religious rites (cp. Hos.
4.12-14) but it came to mean a breach of Israel's covenant faith.
The phrase AFTER THE GODS OF STRANGERS (A.V.) should read
'after strange gods'. The word 'strange' occurs only here
and in 32.12 in Deuteronomy. It literally means 'foreign'

and then comes to have a deeper meaning. In v. 19 WRITE YE associates Joshua with Moses in the Song (as also 32.44). The word 'imagination' (Hebrew *Yetser*), which in itself may be either good or bad, is often applied in the Old Testament to evil imagination in rebellion against God (cp. Gen. 6.5, 8.21, Ps. 10.2, 140.2, Prov. 6.18, Lam. 3.60) and the doctrine of the evil imagination, the *yetser ha ra$^c$* has played an important part in the later theology of the problem of evil.[1]

**24-26** come from a later tradition which justifies the setting aside of the Deuteronomic legislation as a working basis of Israel's life, while keeping it in a place of honour among the traditions of Israel. The Levites, here used in the later sense, are to put it with the ark (cp. 10.8-9). The fact that the Deuteronomic law was to be read in the year of release, and that this law was not practised, helped to bring about its supersession by the later laws, before the whole Pentateuch became binding on Judaism.

In vv. 27-29 Moses again speaks of the rebellion and certain corruption of Israel. If they have been rebellious in his lifetime (cp. 1.26.43, 9.6-7.13.23-24, 10.16) how much more will they be when he is not there to control them? So he speaks the words of the Song to Israel assembled under its officers as a witness against them. It is a harsh judgment upon the history of Israel by a later time. It may be a condemnation of Northern Israel by the school of Chronicles.

### 32.1-44  The Song of Moses: A Psalm on the Coming Victory of God

This poem has no connection with the time of Moses, though as a poetic expression of the theme of Deuteronomy, it is not out of place. It refers to the Exodus as days of old (v. 7), it describes Israel as in a state of idolatry (6-18) and defeat (30), its deliverance (36-43) is in the future. The affinities of the poem are with Jeremiah, Ezekiel and Deutero-Isaiah, but no mention of exile occurs in it. It may come from the traditions of the Northern Kingdom before it went into captivity to Assyria, but it seems best to put it in the time of Jeremiah and

[1] cp. N. P. Williams: *The Ideas of the Fall and Original Sin*, pp. 59-70.

Ezekiel (about 630 B.C.). The poem is not comparable with the masterpieces of Hebrew poetry, but as a didactic psalm, it has a fire and sweep unequalled in the Old Testament. (For its general plan cp. Ps. 78, 105, 106, and Ezek. 16, 20, 23. This didactic psalm may be contrasted with the lyric hymn called the Song of Moses in Ex. 15.1-21. cp. Rev. 15.3.)

1-3 Introduction: The Greatness of God
4-6 The faithfulness of God and the folly of Israel
7-14 God's care for Israel
15-18 The ingratitude of Israel
19-25 The just punishment of Israel
26-27 Vengeance on Israel withheld
28-30 Israel abandoned by God
31-33 The corruption of Israel's enemies
34-36 God's vengeance is at hand!
37-39 The folly of trust in other gods
40-42 The promise of vengeance on Israel's foes
43 Conclusion: Rejoice with Israel in their coming vindication by God

**1-3.** The poet appeals to heaven and earth, not as witnesses against Israel, but as listeners to his great theme, who themselves are dependent on the reality of God. The message given to him is to drop like rain and like dew upon ground thirsty for it. Its purpose is to waken trust in the living God. His theme is the character of God, manifested in dealings with Israel, and what Israel can hope from him.

**4-6.** God is utterly dependable in a world infected with change and decay. He is the Rock, on which Israel is secure. The God of Israel is righteous. All his ways are judgment, he is a God of faithfulness, just and right is he. Israel have corrupted themselves. They are a perverse and crooked generation. This is a stupid response to God's fatherly care.

The word ROCK is used six times of God in this poem. S. R. Driver says: 'It designates Jehovah by a forcible and expressive figure, as the unchangeable support or refuge of his servants, and is used with evident appropriateness where the thought is of God's unvarying attitude towards his people. The figure is, no doubt, like crag, stronghold, high place, etc.,

derived from the natural scenery of Palestine.' Compare also
II Sam. 23.3, Isa. 17.10, 30.29 R.V., Hab. 1.12 R.V., Ps. 18.
2.31.46, 19.14 R.V., 28.1. The most important uses of the
term 'rock' in the New Testament are its ascription to Peter
(Matt. 16.18); the application of the term 'rock of offence' to
Christ (Rom. 9.33); and St. Paul's assertion that the water-
giving rock, which, according to Jewish legend, accompanied
the Israelites in the wilderness, was Christ (I Cor. 10.4).

In v. 5 the true Hebrew text is uncertain. In v. 6 for A.V.
BOUGHT read 'begotten'.

**7-14.** The traditions of Israel are quite clear and definite:
they testify to the unwavering care by God of Israel. Among
the nations Israel is Yahweh's inheritance. He found Israel
in the wilderness and took care of him. He gave him confidence to go forward as a vulture teaches her young to fly. He
alone did this for Israel. He gave Israel triumphant and
undisputed possession of the new land to enjoy its rich
fertility.

**8.** The meaning of the last clause is uncertain; read either
with T. J. Meek 'He assigned the realms of the nations to
various deities' or with the Bible in Basic English 'he had the
limits of the peoples marked out, keeping in mind the number
of the children of Israel'. In v. 10 the apple of the eye is the
pupil (Heb. 'the little man'). The poet starts with the wilderness as providing the most effective contrast with Israel's in-
gratitude (cp. Hos. 9.10, Ezek. 16.3-6). The illustration of
the eagle (properly the vulture) mentioned in Ex. 19.4 is here
developed to show how Yahweh has given his people confidence. The bird stirs the young out of the nest, but then hovers
about them, and when they are unable or too tired to fly,
catches them on her own back. This is how God has cared for
his people (cp. 1.31 and Hos. 11.1.3 and also Luke 13.34).

**13.** He made him ride on the high places of the earth (cp.
the promise in Isa. 58.14). Wheeler Robinson says: 'The
figure is that of the victorious warrior advancing resistlessly
(33.29; Hab. 3.19; Ps. 18.33), and is elsewhere applied to
Yahweh himself (Amos 4.13, Micah 1.3), who makes his child
sharer in his victory.' In v. 14 after RAMS read: 'herds of

Bashan and goats, with the very choicest wheat, and the blood of the grapes, a foaming draught'. (T. J. Meek.)

**15-18.** But Israel sated itself in the gifts, and forgot and forsook the giver. They provoked him to intolerance of other allegiances, and anger at the evil ways. They sacrificed to devils, to no-gods, and to new gods, whom their fathers did not reverence. Of the motherly affection of God their Rock they were unmindful.

**15.** Before this verse the Samaritan version and the Septuagint have 'And Jacob ate and was full' which suits the sense. 'Jeshurun' means the upright one (33.5.26, Isa. 44.2). v. 15 for A.V. LIGHTLY ESTEEMED read 'treated as a fool'. (George Adam Smith says: 'How often in their superstition men act as if God could be tricked, and in their immorality as if He were senseless.')

**16.** Strange gods (lit. strangers) cp. Jer. 2.25, 3.13.

**17.** See on v. 21. v. 18 for A.V. BEGAT read 'bare' and for A.V. FORMED THEE read 'was in travail with thee'.

**19-25.** Yahweh saw the contempt of his people, and spurned them, hiding his face from them because of their faithlessness. He determined to support a worthless people, a no people, to make his own people intolerant of the favour this people have with God and angry at their triumph. God's anger which burns down to the underworld shall blaze against his people, and evils shall be heaped upon them.

**19.** For A.V. ABHORRED read 'spurned'. v. 20. Sin results in God hiding his face (cp. 31.17, Isa. 57.17). For A.V. FROWARD read 'uncontrolled', for FAITH read 'steadfastness'. v. 21. As men have done, so it shall be dealt to them. For no-gods see Jer. 2.11, 5.7, 16.20, II Chron. 13.9.

**17** and **21** are used by St. Paul in two passages. In Rom. 10.19 and 11.11 he finds the salvation of the Gentiles, which has become clear to him through the fact of Christ, plainly stated in the Old Testament. The Gentiles are the no-people who are to provoke Israel to a new love and loyalty to God. James Denney says: [2] 'The very calling of the Gentiles, predicted and interpreted as it is in the passages quoted, should

[2] *Expositor's Greek Testament*, II, 674-5.

itself have been a message to the Jews, which they could not misunderstand; it should have opened their eyes as with a lightning flash to the position in which they stood—that of men who had forfeited their place among the people of God— and provoked them out of jealousy, to vie with these outsiders in welcoming the righteousness of faith.'

Also in I Cor. 10.20-22, Paul insists that Christian believers cannot drink the cup of the Lord and the cup of devils, i.e. no gods. To do this is to repeat that sin of God's people which made God jealous, i.e. intolerant of a divided loyalty. James Moffatt writes:[3] 'The tragic failures of ancient Israel had been due to the fact that, either under the strain of life or owing to the fascinations of paganism, the people had been tempted to think that the Lord with whom they were in fellowship was not enough; he had either to be replaced or supplemented. In the present paragraph Paul continues this warning against the divided heart. The Lord of our fellowship must have our unshared allegiance.'

In v. 22 for A.V. INTO THE LOWEST HELL read 'to the depths of the underworld' (Heb. *Sheol*).

In v. 24 the true Hebrew text is uncertain. On this verse cp. the four sore plagues of Ezek. 14.21.

**26-27.** God would even have destroyed Israel as a people for their sin, were it not that he feared that the enemies would attribute this not to the action of God himself but to their own superior strength. Adam Welch says,[4] 'God could not surrender Israel to which He had revealed His mind and which He had made His instrument to His larger ends, without surrendering the ends for which he had chosen it. He would fail Himself, if He failed to maintain those who had committed themselves to Him. What filled the writer's mind and stayed up his own heart was the note with which he opened, the thought of the divine self-consistency. He found in that a clue to the mystery of history and a help to faith in the harsh perplexities of his own time. The world would lose meaning if Israel disappeared.' (cp. 9.28, Ex. 32.12, Num. 14.15-16, and

[3] *Moffatt Commentary*, p. 137.
[4] *Deuteronomy: the Framework to the Code*, p. 148.

on the thought *for his name's sake* Isa. 48.9-11, Jer. 14.7.21, Ezek. 20.9.14.22; 36.21-38.)

**28-30.** It is a sign of the stupidity of Israel that they cannot realize that their present intentions can lead only to disaster (cp. Jer. 5.31). How could they be so easily defeated unless God, their Rock, had given them up to the enemy. v. 30 for A.V. SHUT read with R.V. 'delivered'.

**31-33.** This defeat of Israel cannot be due to the gods of Israel's enemies, because, as they have been obliged to admit (cp. Ex. 14.25, Num. 23-24, Josh. 2.9-11, I Sam. 4.8, 5.7.10-11; I Kings 20.23-30) Yahweh the God of Israel is stronger than their Gods. It cannot be the peoples themselves because they are of the same stock as the people of Sodom and Gomorrah, and deserve destruction. In v. 32 for A.V. GALL read ' poison '. In v. 33 for POISON OF DRAGONS read ' venom of serpents ', and for VENOM OF ASPS read ' poison of cobras '.

**34-36.** But the day of God's vengeance is at hand! This is good news for Israel. He shall vindicate his own people when their strength has gone. v. 34 for A.V. TREASURES read with R.V. marg. ' treasuries '. v. 35 for A.V. TO ME BELONGETH VENGEANCE and R.V. ' vengeance is mine ' read with the Samaritan version and the Septuagint ' for the day of vengeance '. For A.V. THEIR FOOT SHALL ABIDE IN DUE TIME read ' for the time when their foot shall slip '. v. 36 JUDGE here means 'vindicate'. For A.V. NONE SHUT UP OR LEFT read ' neither bound nor free are left '. On the thought of God's vengeance, which is commoner in the later prophets than in the earlier ones see Isa. 1.24, Micah 5.15, Neh. 1.2, Ezek. 25.14.17; Jer. 5.9.29; 9.9, 46.10, 50.15.28; 51.6, 11; Isa. 34.8, 35.4, 47.3, 59.17, 61.2, 63.4.

The Hebrew of v. 35 VENGEANCE IS MINE is quoted in Hebrews and in Romans for two different purposes. In Heb. 10.30 the passage (including v. 36) is interpreted as declaring God's punishment of his people for their sins. The repudiation of the greater salvation given in Christ will surely receive greater punishment. They will fall outside the range of God's mercy under his retribution. By the standard of the New Testament as a whole, this writer's thought is limited in

M

(1) not laying sufficient emphasis on the persistence of divine grace, and (2) not emphasizing that the retribution of God is intended to be an instrument of his saving mercy.

In Rom. 12.19 Paul exhorts Christian people to leave retribution to God and practise unwearying goodwill to those who treat them with evil. This passage does not solve the problem of how far retribution is a process in a moral universe which God permits but which does not represent his deliberate purpose, and which therefore should not be imitated. It is quite clear that retribution is not the distinctive Christian emphasis in conduct, but it also seems clear that in the public life of the world it can be under-emphasized as well as over-emphasized.

**37-39.** Yahweh shall say: ' Where are the gods that they have turned to as their support and their security instead of me? Where are the gods on whom they have lavished all their devotion? Let them help and protect them now.' Let Israel recognize in its extremity that Yahweh is the true God, by himself alone. He has power of life and death, of wounding and healing, he has incontestable authority over all the world.

Dr. Welch says,[5] ' The insolence of the heathen has not been directed against the nation which acknowledged him: it was levelled against him and his just government of the world. He should vindicate that government and in the act vindicate those who through evil report and good had clung to faith in its permanence.'

God, who had brought Israel to its present state of need, can, if it is his purpose to do so, bring upon Israel new prosperity. This is what Israel must believe (cp. Isa. 41.4, 43.10-13, 45.6-7, 48.12; see also Luke 12.4-5).

**40-42.** God will take vengeance on his enemies. The enemies are, of course, the victorious heathen who have been afflicting Israel. S. R. Driver says, ' Jehovah's vengeance is pictured as accomplished amidst a scene of carnage, such as the Hebrew prophets, especially the later ones, love to imagine ' (e.g. Isa. 34.5-6, 49.26, 63.3-6, 66.16, Jer. 12.12, 25.30-33,

---

[5] *Deuteronomy: the Framework to the Code*, pp. 145-6.

46.10, 50.25-29). v. 42 for A.V. FROM THE BEGINNING OF
REVENGES UPON THE ENEMY read 'from the long-haired heads
of the enemy'.

**43.** All nations are to congratulate Israel on their God,
who will make up for the suffering of his people, and take
vengeance on his enemies and make the promised land holy.
In the last clause of v. 43 for A.V. BE MERCIFUL UNTO HIS
LAND, AND TO HIS PEOPLE read 'clear from guilt the land of his
people'. Heb. 1.6 quotes a Septuagint addition to the Hebrew
text of this verse—let the angels of God worship him—the
angels as well as the surrounding nations being summoned
to pay homage to Yahweh. There it is applied to the Son.
In Rom. 15.10 Paul uses the opening words of this verse,
among other quotations, to move the Gentile Christians to
glorify God for his mercy in calling them too into his kingdom.

**44.** In the editorial note Joshua is associated with Moses
in the Song.

The message of the Song is a message of encouragement
and hope in the fundamental relations between God and man.

It speaks first of God's care for his people. Here the
theme is God's care for his people in the wilderness. For the
Christian the supreme act of God's care for us is his act of
redemption in the life, death, and resurrection of Jesus Christ.
But this central act of God's caring must be linked with God's
care of our own life, and our assurance, in spite of anything
that has happened to us, that he watches over us.

It also speaks of the suffering brought by sin. We have
learnt from the rest of the Bible that the mystery of suffering
is more complicated than this, and that suffering is often not
in the least punishment for sin. Some suffering comes because
we are trying to do God's will, and some suffering we must
be content to bear without explanation in fellowship with
God. We must constantly remember that we cannot do justice
to the mystery of suffering except in the light of the Cross of
Christ, and our understanding of the meaning of that Cross
must be strong and deep. It is important in the modern world,
which has made so plain the fact that the process of life is
complicated, that we should admit that the effect of sin is

pervasive and corrosive in spoiling God's gift of life to us. The unfaithfulness of his people before God is the largest part of our real unhappiness.

The Song also speaks of retribution—the frustration of evil purposes and the victory of God's purposes. It does so in harsh and cruel terms, as though God exulted in slaughter. In the light of Christ, as well as of the greatest moments of the Old Testament itself, we cannot admit this. But in principle the retribution of God is real and necessary. Evil cannot always be triumphant: it is part of God's purpose that it should be frustrated. The triumph of God must become real, and all that opposes that purpose must lose its power.

The victory of God is at hand! It takes courage in the midst of an indifferent and unbelieving generation to affirm the reality of God as a factor in our present life. God as part of a never-interfering background is one thing; God as changing the situation in which we stand is another. Here the psalmist speaks to us. We need to enter into the confident affirmation of the Bible that the victory of God is at hand, and in fellowship with Christ, to awake to its meaning to-day.

### 32.45-47   Moses commends the law as Israel's life

Moses again exhorts Israel to listen to all the words of the law and see that their children obey it, for it is their life, and by it their days in the land will be prolonged. This passage is Deuteronomic, and may fittingly be connected with 31.9-13. The keeping of the law and the love of God are virtually identified (cp. 30.20). We have to remember that in the Old Testament *Torah* (Law or Instruction) is as much a gift of God and a sign of his empowering grace as a demand from men. This is true, even though we should read in v. 46 'the words which I testify against you' (instead of A.V. AMONG YOU). The law is a witness against human sin. IT IS YOUR LIFE. Who can set limits to the enrichment and freedom of life which would take place if our nations set as the foundation of its moral and material well-being the love of God with heart and mind and soul and strength?

## 32.48-52 Moses is called to die on Mount Nebo

Moses is ordered to climb Mount Nebo and see the land of Canaan which God is giving Israel for a possession. He shall die there, as Aaron on Mount Hor because of their sin at Kadesh. But though Moses shall not enter the Promised Land he shall see it.

This passage comes from the later tradition and is an expanded duplicate of Num. 27.2-14. Pisgah is Deuteronomy's word for Mount Nebo (see 3.27), and the two are identified in 34.1. On Mount Hor see Num. 20.22-29. In 10.6 the place of Aaron's death is said to be Mosera. The account of the sin of Moses and Aaron mentioned here and of Aaron's death is given in Num. 20.2-29. In v. 52 for A.V. BEFORE THEE read 'from a distance'.

## 33.1-29 The Blessing of Moses—a Poem on God and the People of God

This poem has no connection with the book of Deuteronomy, into which it has been inserted because of the connection of both with the Northern Kingdom. It is much later than Moses, and breathes an atmosphere of prosperity and confidence in the settled Kingdom. The date is probably that of the reign of Jeroboam I (931-911 B.C.), though some scholars have put it as late as that of the reign of Jeroboam II (783-743 B.C.). (The opening theme and conclusion form a single poem, which may be later than the blessing of the tribes, but which was linked with that from a very early time.) It is to be compared with the Blessing of Jacob (Gen. 49.2-27), the corresponding poem coming from the Southern Kingdom, which is earlier (' it took final shape in the age of David or Solomon' (i.e. 1000-970 B.C.), Skinner) and much less religious in tone than the poem in Deuteronomy. It is also to be compared with the Song of Deborah (Judg. 5) (which is 'the oldest extant monument of Hebrew literature, and the only contemporaneous monument of Hebrew history before the foundation of the Kingdom' (Moore)), and with the poems attributed to Balaam in Num. 23 and 24 (which were composed in the time of Saul and David to which they refer and are pervaded by a 'feeling

of national confidence, success, prosperity and contentment'
(Gray)).

**1.** The term MAN OF GOD, though used frequently of prophets
in I Sam., I and II Kings, is only used of Moses here, Josh. 14.6
and in the title of Ps. 90. A blessing in ancient belief had
power to bring about what it affirmed.

**2-5.** Yahweh revealed himself to Israel, and established
himself as their king. While the general meaning is clear, the
Hebrew text is corrupt, and the details are quite uncertain.
The passage may have been influenced by the Song of Deborah
(cp. also Heb. 3). In v. 2 SINAI is put for Deuteronomy's
word 'Horeb'. For A.V. ROSE UP read 'beamed'. For A.V.
WITH TEN THOUSAND OF SAINTS read 'to Meribath-Kadesh'.
The translation 'with holy myriads' is the source of the later
belief that the law was ordained through angels (Acts 7.50,
Gal. 3.19, Heb. 2.2). For A.V. A FIERY LAW read a 'burning
fire'. God has come up from the south, where his dwelling
is, giving light like the sun to help his people.

In v. 3 read 'he loves his people'. The meaning of the
rest of the verse is very uncertain. In v. 4 MOSES COMMANDED
US A LAW is probably an intrusion, which seeks to connect this

revealing activity with the giving of the law at Horeb. v. 5 JESHURUN, that is, Israel, the upright one, as 32.15.

**6.** May Reuben keep its existence 'but not be numerous' is the meaning, and not the A.V. AND LET NOT HIS MEN BE FEW. S. R. Driver says: 'The dwindling numbers and national insignificance of the tribe are reflected in the blessing.'

**7.** Bring Judah back to his people Israel and help him in his difficulties. This is the Northern Kingdom's view of Judah after the separation of the Kingdoms; contrast the space and importance attached to Judah in Gen. 49.8-12. For A.V. LET HIS HANDS BE SUFFICIENT FOR HIM read 'with thy hands contend for him'.

Simeon is not mentioned here. It has been suggested that the first part of v. 7 should apply to Simeon and the second part of v. 7 and v. 11 should apply to Judah (see Moffatt's translation). But this is unlikely. Simeon was absorbed in the territory of Judah at an early date.

**8-11.** Levi is God's priestly tribe who have proved their impartiality. He tells Israel God's judgments and offers his sacrifices. May God destroy his enemies! This is in marked contrast to Gen. 29.5-7 where Simeon and Levi as secular tribes are condemned for their cruelty. Thummim and Urim, usually mentioned in the reverse order (see I Sam. 14.41, Ex. 28.30, Lev. 8.8, Ezra 2.63, Neh. 7.65), were the two sacred lots used by the priests in giving decisions, probably to indicate yes or no. We know nothing of Massah (Ex. 17.1-7) and Meribah (Num. 20.2-13) which would connect Levi with them or make such connection stand to his credit. v. 9 evidently refers to Levi's power of resisting the claim of family ties in doing justice in Israel. For A.V. HIM read 'them'. In v. 10 for A.V. INCENSE read 'sweet smoke' (of sacrifice). We do not know who the enemies of Levi are—probably they are non-Levitical priests still maintaining themselves at some of the sanctuaries.

**12.** Benjamin is God's beloved; he watches over him and dwells in his midst. This contrasts vividly with Gen. 49 where Benjamin is praised for his wolf-like fierceness. The tenses of the verb are present. For SHALL COVER read 'shatters'.

The place of the sanctuary of God in Benjamin is disputed. Ultimately, of course, it was Jerusalem.

**13-17.** Joseph—that is Ephraim and Manasseh—is praised for his fertility and military achievements. This follows much the same lines as in Gen. 49.22-26, except that Joseph has been hard-pressed militarily but in the end has been successful. In these passages the favour of Israel's God is essential and as natural and inevitable a source of fertility as the rain above or the springs in the earth. In the passage for FOR read 'with', and for PRECIOUS THINGS OR FRUITS read 'wealth'. v. 14, for FOR THE DEW read 'above'.

**16.** On THE GOODWILL OF HIM THAT DWELT IN THE BUSH Dillmann says: 'God, by an advance beyond Gen. 49.24-25 (where God is called the God of Jacob), is designated emblematically as the God of the Mosaic covenant.' It is interesting that this is the one passage in the Old Testament where the revelation of God in the burning bush is mentioned, and that our Lord picks out the passage (Ex. 3.1-6) to use in his affirmation that those whom God has taken into fellowship with himself have entered upon a life that is eternal (Mark 12.18-27, Luke 20.27-40). The Revelation of God in the bush is also mentioned in Stephen's speech in Acts. 7.30-35.

**16-17.** For A.V. THAT WAS SEPARATED FROM read with R.V. marg. 'that is prince among'. For A.V. HIS GLORY IS LIKE THE FIRSTLING OF HIS BULLOCK read with R.V. marg. 'His firstling bullock, majesty is his', i.e. Ephraim. For A.V. UNICORNS read with R.V. 'the wild-ox'; the strength of Ephraim is exaggerated in the suggestion that even the ends of the earth must feel the power of his horns. Dr. Welch says: [*] 'Manasseh was sufficiently distinct from Ephraim to deserve separate mention, though it had clearly become second in importance to its powerful neighbour.'

**18-19.** Zebulun and Issachar are praised for their prosperity in trade. Zebulun must have had an outlet to the sea (cp. Gen. 49.13) and Issachar be prosperous in its inland trade (contrast Gen. 49.14-15 where Issachar is blamed for its inability to maintain its independence). The call of the peoples is

[*] *Deuteronomy: the Framework to the Code*, p. 123.

to share in a religious festival and fair. This would have been condemned by later legislation. The term SACRIFICES OF RIGHTEOUSNESS, the meaning of which is capable of expansion, is found only here and in Psalms 4.5 and 51.19. TREASURES HID IN THE SAND probably refer to the use of sand in the making of glass.

**20-21.** God has enlarged the territory of Gad who is commended for his military prowess (cp. Gen. 49.19) and for his help in fulfilling Yahweh's purpose for Israel. v. 21 for A.V. PROVIDED FOR HIMSELF read 'chose'. The territory of God was among the first to be occupied. For A.V. BECAUSE THERE, IN A PORTION OF THE LAWGIVER WAS HE SEATED read with R.V. marg. 'for there was a ruler's portion reserved'. The Hebrew text is very uncertain. In the latter part of v. 21 Gad is praised for helping in the conquest of Canaan.

**22.** Dan is praised for his military achievement. The phrase 'a lion's whelp' is applied in Gen. 49 to Judah, where Dan is referred to as a serpent surprising the traveller.

**23.** S. R. Driver says: 'Naphtali, blessed as it is with nature's gifts through Jehovah's favour (v. 16), is not to be limited to the highland plateau (the hill country of Naphtali, Josh. 20.7) of Upper Galilee, well watered and richly wooded as it is: it is to possess in addition the yet more fertile and beautiful region, exuberant with an almost tropical vegetation, which borders on the lake of Gennesaret.' For A.V. THE WEST read 'the sea'.

**24-25.** May Asher be specially favoured in Israel and be rich in oil and have strength to resist his enemies. For A.V. WITH CHILDREN read with R.V. marg. 'above sons'. The olive trees of Galilee were famous. v. 25 for A.V. SHOES read 'bolts'. In its position on the north coast Asher needed to be able to defend itself. The poet prays that Asher's strength may never decline.

**26-29.** The God of Israel is absolutely unique. Israel's security comes from living in him and knowing his support. He has destroyed their enemies. Israel dwells unmolested in a fertile land. Israel shares in the uniqueness of their God and other nations shall know it. Matthew Henry says: 'Moses . . .

magnifies both the God of Israel and the Israel of God. They
are both incomparable in his eye.' That is a free summary of
this concluding affirmation of faith. v. 26 for A.V. EXCEL-
LENCY read 'exaltation'. On v. 27 S. R. Driver says: 'Not
only is God a dwelling place (Ps. 90.1) for his people, He is also
their unfailing support; His almighty arms are ever beneath
them, bearing them up, and sustaining them, alike in their
prosperity and their need.' For the figure compare Hos. 11.3,
Isa. 33.2, 51.5, Ps. 44.3, 89.21. In vv. 27 and 28 omit the
word 'shall'. v. 29 for A.V. SHALL BE FOUND LIARS UNTO
THEE read with T. J. Meek, 'shall come cringing to thee'.

Dr. Welch says[7] that the poem of chap. 32 'has a character
which has practically disappeared from modern life. To understand it, it is necessary to go back to a time when men could
worship together as naturally as they fought side by side. To
its author the faith which made Israel a nation and which was
the rich source of its exuberant and hopeful vitality was like a
flag. He could exult as heartily in the achievement of his
people and in every part of its exuberant life as he did in the
knowledge that this was based on the faith which only Israel
could acknowledge. . . . The other documents have a flavour
of the seminary about them. And the seminary, whether it is
prophetic or priestly in its character, always remains the
seminary. Chap. 33 leaves the impression of having been written in the open air.'

This poem is concerned not with the church of Israel but
with the nation of Israel. It speaks of the public life of Israel
and refers it all to God. The details of the poem are not prescribed by God but by what has happened to Israel. As between
Gen. 49 and Deut. 33 the details change, but in good times and
in bad times the national life needs to be brought into touch
with God.

The poem deals with the kind of material with which Lord
Mayors, Mayors, and Chairmen of County Councils have
constantly to deal—the public life of the community. We are
the poorer in our modern life if we cannot mix God easily and
naturally with the happenings of day to day. One of the

[7] *Deuteronomy: the Framework to the Code*, p. 125.

reasons why we find it hard to do this, is that we have grown fastidious and afraid to link God with what might merit his condemnation. How shall we link our present prosperity or escape from evil with God's will, when, if only we knew all the factors at work we would know that it is neither good in itself nor beneficial? There is a true perception here, but it can be wrongly exaggerated. It is worse through fastidiousness to leave our ordinary life unrelated to the eternity of God than to make blunders by seeing the action of God in the wrong places. The public life of mankind needs the context of God, if it is to be true to itself.

The opening theme, in spite of the corruption of the text, is clear and drives us back on to the Deuteronomic exposition of the first commandment. The poem rejoices in the security and prosperity of Israel. It is characteristic not merely of the poem, but of the Bible as a whole, to find the origin of that security and prosperity in God. This raises insistently for the modern mind the question: can we afford to neglect the first and great commandment—to love the Lord our God with heart and mind and soul and strength—as though our failure to obey it left life unchanged?

The concluding verses express clearly, if in limited and partly distorted form, the theme of the whole Bible, God, and the people of God. Because God is incomparable, therefore his people share in some of his characteristic quality. It is not merely the great word—THE ETERNAL GOD IS THY REFUGE AND UNDERNEATH ARE THE EVERLASTING ARMS which should hold us: it is the expression of that essential message on which, deepened, broadened, and purified, we all depend. God leads us to discover his incomparable greatness that from our life in him we may be willing to be made into the true greatness of the people of God.

### 34.1-12 The Death of Moses. His place in the History of Israel

This chapter is the gathering together of many sources and traditions not all mutually compatible. It is probable that there were different traditions about the place from which

Moses viewed the Promised Land and about the place of his death. OVER AGAINST JERICHO (v. 1) is not the same as OVER AGAINST BETH-PEOR (v. 6). The historical reality, here as elsewhere, was a little more complicated than it is represented to be.

Moses went to the mountain, here called both PISGAH (the Deuteronomic word) and NEBO (the word of later tradition) as God had commanded him (3.27, 32.49). And God showed him the land into which his people were to go. The possibilities are somewhat exaggerated, but a spacious view of the land is certainly possible. In v. 1 for A.V. ALL THE LAND OF GILEAD UNTO DAN read ' all the land—Gilead as far as Dan '. In v. 2 THE UTMOST SEA is, of course, the western sea—the Mediterranean.

George Adam Smith describes the need for and possibility of this view into the Promised Land as follows,[8] ' During their journey over the table-land, Israel had no outlook westward over the Dead Sea. For westward the Plateau rises a little and shuts out all view.' Nebo is a headland ' almost certainly that which breaks from the Plateau half-way between Heshbon and Mâdeba, and runs out, under the name of Neba, nearly opposite the north end of the Dead Sea.' This is the view from it. ' The whole of the Jordan Valley is now open from Engedi, beyond which the mists become impenetrable, to where, on the north, the hills of Gilead seem to meet those of Ephraim. The Jordan flows below: Jericho is visible beyond. Over Gilead, Hermon can be seen in clear weather, but the heat hid it from us. The view is almost that described as the last on which the eyes of Moses rested, the higher hills of Western Palestine shutting out the possibility of a sight of the sea.'

This is the land promised to Abraham, Isaac and Jacob (cp. e.g. Ex. 33.1, Deut. 1.8) which Moses can see but not enter.

So Moses, the servant of Yahweh (Ex. 14.31, Num. 12.7-8, Josh. 1.1.13.15, 8.31, I Kings 8.53.56, II Kings 21.8, Mal. 4.4, Ps. 105.26, I Chron. 6.49, II Chron. 1.3, 24.6-9, Neh. 1.7-8, 9.14, 10.29, Dan. 9.11) died in Moab according to God's word.

[8] *A Historical Geography of the Holy Land*, pp. 592-3.

Adam Welch says:[9] 'What the writer wished to emphasize was that Moses did nòt die through sickness or old age. This great servant of the Lord died without entering the land of promise, died because it was the divine will. God, who had called him into His service and endowed him with the gifts for its fulfilment, had the right and power to decide when that service was fulfilled.'

And God buried Moses but no man knows the burying-place. (A legend connected with this is mentioned in Jude 9.) George Adam Smith says:[10] 'Between the streams, that in these valleys spring full-born from the rocks, and the merry corn-fields·on the Plateau above, are some thousand feet of slopes and gullies, where no foot comès, the rock is crumbling, and silence reigns save for the west wind moaning through the thistles. Here Moses was laid. Who would wish to know the exact spot? The whole region is a sepulchre.'

And Moses' life spanned three generations, and when he died, his vitality was not exhausted. This is a natural tribute by a later generation to the tremendous energy of Moses. Martin Buber says:[11] 'He was an aged man. But as he stands upon the peak everything within him demonstrates the soul that has not aged. His eyes were not dimmed, and his freshness had not fled; that is the speech of a people's memory.'

And Israel mourned for Moses for thirty days, (as for Aaron, Num. 20.29) and obeyed Joshua who had been com-missioned by Moses, and did as Yahweh had commanded Moses. The SPIRIT OF WISDOM is the practical ability of leadership. Its full meaning is given in Isa. 11.2. In Num. 27.18-23 Joshua already has the spirit before Moses lays hands on him. Joshua had his own gift from God—the fulness of his own call Moses could not transmit. This is a late tradition, but the' principle is right. The great leader is dead, but there is something more important than the great leader. The Lord's work must go on, and it is a tribute to his greatness that it does.

[9] *Deuteronomy: the Framework to the Code*, p. 186.
[10] *op. cit.*, pp. 594-5.
[11] *Moses*, p. 201.

In the history of Israel Moses is incomparably the greatest prophet because of the intimacy of his communion with God (see Ex. 33.11, Num. 12.6-8) and because of the almighty deeds which were the fruit of that communion. ' These closing words of the Book of Deuteronomy,' writes Mr. Winston Churchill,[12] ' are an apt expression of the esteem in which the great leader and liberator of the Hebrew people was held by the generations that succeeded him.'

W. A. L. Elmslie says:[13] ' Moses succeeded. There is the tremendous fact that the whole story was told so as to exalt the work of God not the glory of Moses. Who but Moses instilled conviction that the Hebrews were to look to their God for salvation, and to think of himself only as the servant of God? Surely that is authentic memory of a great man seen to be living for an end greater than himself? Moses succeeded in his *essential* task. When the Hebrews crossed over Jordan, there were some who understood that to worship Yahweh as God was to worship One whose amazing might was actuated by amazing mercy.'

In the story of the Transfiguration (Mark 9.2-8, Matt. 17.1-8, Luke 9.28-36) Elijah is associated with Moses in talking with Jesus about the departure which he was to accomplish at Jerusalem. ' By thus appearing together,' says A. M. Ramsey,[14] ' Moses and Elijah sum up the entire drama of the old order from its beginning to its end—the one is the predecessor, the other is the precursor of the Messiah.' This is the traditional estimate of the Old Testament, with which the New Testament works. We cannot think exactly like this to-day. The greatness of Moses after being minimized is being reaffirmed, and we are constrained to affirm that the root of the characteristic quality of Israel's faith goes back to the mission entrusted to him; but we must associate with him (as of equal importance for the fulfilling of God's purpose for Israel) those prophets who enabled Israel to use the exiles that came upon them for a deeper, grander, and more abiding fellowship with God.

[12] ' Moses—the leader of a people ' in *Thoughts and Adventures*, 1932.
[13] *How came our faith?* pp. 222-3.
[14] *The Glory of God and the Transfiguration of Christ*, p. 114.

And all—even Moses—are subordinate to the supreme figure of Israel's history and of the world's history—the incarnate Son of God. In him a greater than Moses is present (cp. John 1.17, II Cor. 3.7-8, Heb. 3.3-6). But in the light of Christ the work of Moses is not set aside, or repudiated, but seen in its true greatness, and welcomed as a means of growth in the knowledge and love of God by them which are in Christ Jesus. Thanks be to God for his servant Moses!